D1579462

Planting
Plans
for your garden

Planting
Plans
for your garden

Jenny Shukman

Guild of Master Craftsman Publications

First published 2001 by
Guild of Master Craftsman Publications Ltd
166 High Street, Lewes
East Sussex, BN7 1XU

Text © Jenny Shukman 2001
© in the Work GMC Publications Ltd

Photographic credits on page 140.

Full colour illustrations © Melanie Clitheroe based on line
drawings by Jenny Shukman: pp. 18–19, 26–7, 30–1, 34–5,
40–1, 46–7, 52–3, 58–9, 62–3, 68–9, 72–3, 76–7, 84–5, 92–3,
98–9, 106–7, 110–11, 114–15, 122–3, 126–7, 130–1 and 134–5.

Colour illustrations of techniques by John Yates: pp. 6, 7–9,
11, 12, 13, 24, 42, 86, 87, 101 and 102.

Black and white planting plans and individual plant
studies © Jenny Shukman.

ISBN 1 86108 199 5

All rights reserved

British Cataloguing in Publication Data.
A catalogue record of this book is available from the
British Library

The right of Jenny Shukman to be identified as the author of
this work has been asserted in accordance with the Copyright
Designs and Patents Act 1988, Sections 77 and 78.

No part of this publication may be reproduced, stored in a
retrieval system, or transmitted in any form or by any means
without the prior permission of the publisher and copyright
owner.

This book is sold subject to the condition that all designs are
copyright and are not for commercial reproduction without
the permission of the designer and copyright owner.

The publishers and authors can accept no legal responsibility
for any consequences arising from the application of
information, advice or instructions given in this publication.

Edited by Gill Parris
Cover and book design by Fineline Studios
Typeface: ITC Galliard

Colour separation by Viscan Graphics Pte Ltd (Singapore)
Printed in Hong Kong by H & Y Printing Ltd

To Phil, Anna, Naomi and Wendy

Contents

The Naming of Plants

Plants may be known by their common names but they are classified by their Latin (or botanical) names. This system for naming plants is based on what is termed the binomial system, which was developed by the Swedish botanist Carl von Linné (1707–1778). Each plant is classified by at least two words.

The genus, or first name, refers to a group of plants with similar botanical features. For example: lonicera, which is the Latin name for honeysuckle. The species, or second name, which cannot be used alone, is a descriptive name for the plant, so *Lonicera fragrantissima* describes a very fragrant honeysuckle.

Sometimes you will see a cross between the names. This refers to an interspecific hybrid which is the result of crossing two related species within the same genus. For example: *Abelia × grandiflora*, which is a cross between two different abelias and has larger flowers.

A cultivar, which I have referred to several times in the text, is a change in the species of a cultivated plant. It is produced by plant breeding and selection and may result, for example, in different coloured or larger flowers, disease resistance or variegated foliage. This is written after the species and is not in Latin. For example: *Garrya elliptica* 'James Roof', which has particularly large catkins. When the plant is particularly distinct and further removed from the original species, it is used straight after the genus. For example: *Choisya* 'Aztec Pearl'.

A slight variation in the species which occurs naturally is termed a variety. For example: *Thalictrum aquilegiifolium* var. *album*, which has white flowers instead of the usual purple.

As scientific knowledge increases, it is sometimes necessary to change plant names. To show the older plant name, it may be put in brackets afterwards. For example: *Darmera peltata* (syn. *Peltiphyllum peltatum*).

To enable you to select the correct plants for the plans, Latin names have been used in the plant lists. In some cases common names are given in brackets afterwards, as well. The common names may be more familiar and are frequently interesting and descriptive but, as the same name is often used for different plants, the Latin name is important for correct selection. Vegetables are the exception to this; these are not generally sold by their Latin names, either as seeds or plants, so in this case common names have been used in the plant lists.

Introduction

This is a book of 'off the peg' planting plans to suit a wide range of garden situations, sizes and styles. Depending on the size of your garden, you may find a plan which suits a particular part of the garden, or you may select one to fill the whole garden. Whether you have a sunny, south-facing plot or a cooler, north-facing garden, a heavy clay soil or a chalky soil, there is a plan here for your garden. You may like an old-fashioned, cottage-garden feel, or you may prefer a modern, meadow style of planting. You may opt for a particular colour scheme, or be looking for seasonal interest, while a low-maintenance garden is of great interest to many. The idea is to open up possibilities for your garden which are not only practical, but will give you many years of enjoyment.

Basic gardening techniques are included in Part One, and here you will find advice on choosing essential tools, assessing your plot, marking out beds and borders, preparing and improving your soil, buying plants, planting and aftercare.

Browse through the chapters in Part Two to select a design which both appeals to you and fits your situation – descriptions of plants, and colour illustrations showing impressions of the mature gardens, will help you to choose. Each planting plan is drawn to the same scale of 1:50, i.e. 1cm=50cm or 1in=50in, and shows exact planting positions. Care has been taken in choosing appropriate plants for each plan and this, together with guidance on the number of plants required, will make purchasing easier and prevent expensive mistakes.

Here's to many hours of pleasure choosing and creating your garden, and watching it mature.

Part One

Basic Gardening Techniques

Basic Gardening Techniques

Essential tools

More expensive equipment might make the work quicker, but you only really need a few basic tools to implement the plans in this book. Two of the most essential are the **spade** and **fork**. Choose tools which you find comfortable to handle and which are the right weight for you. Stainless steel tools are long lasting and easy to keep clean, but some may be on the heavy side. Border forks are a useful alternative if you find the full-sized forks too heavy. Smaller-sized spades are also available, and these are perfectly adequate for digging.

Next you need a **rake**, suitable for breaking up and levelling the ground ready for planting or sowing. This should be a general garden rake with short, sturdy teeth. A **trowel** is useful for planting smaller plants, and a **garden line** essential for straight lines for borders or seed drills. A **draw hoe** will make neat and even seed drills. Once the border or garden has been planted out, a **Dutch hoe** is a useful tool for keeping weeds under control. However, care must be taken not to hoe too closely to any shallow rooting plants. A **hand fork** is a useful addition for delicate weeding tasks.

Extras

If you need to start off by clearing and digging a large area, you may consider it a better option to use a **rotary cultivator**. This is a more expensive item of equipment, but hiring is an alternative if you are unlikely to use it a lot afterwards.

When you mark out your new bed or border, you can use a spade. However, if you are cutting into existing turf you can achieve a nice clean edge by using a half-moon-shaped **edging iron**.

A **shredder** is a useful addition if you have a lot of woody prunings to deal with.

A draw hoe

A half-moon-shaped edging iron

A shredder

Assessing your plot

In order to choose a suitable plan for your garden you will need to consider several factors. The plants that may be growing in your garden already, or in neighbouring gardens, will help to give you some idea.

1 First of all, work out in which direction north lies and which areas of the garden are particularly sunny or shady.

2 Next, assess the type of soil you have. A simple way to do this is to feel a handful of moist soil. Clay will feel sticky and you will be able to mould it. The particles are small and fit closely together, making air and water movement difficult in the soil. A well drained, sandy soil will feel gritty to the touch. These particles are larger, allowing good air and water movement, but often causing the soil to dry out quickly. Many soils are a combination of different particles and most of the plans in this book will be suitable. If you have a soil which is at either

extreme much can be done to improve growing conditions, but plans are included for both clay soils and those which are freely draining.

3 Test the pH of your soil. This refers to the acidity or alkalinity of the soil. Again, look at plants which thrive in your area. If plants such as rhododendrons, heathers and camellias are growing well, your soil is likely to be acid. Soils overlying chalk are likely to be pale in appearance, shallow and stony, and will be alkaline. Simple pH meters and test kits are available at many garden centres and DIY stores. Take several readings at different points in your garden for a more accurate picture. An ideal for most plants is about 6.5, but a wide range of plants will grow between 5.5 and 7.5. It is an uphill battle to change extremes of pH, so opt for an appropriate plan.

4 Consider how much time you wish to spend looking after your garden once it is established. If time is in short supply, opt for a low maintenance plan with shrubs that are easy to care for. If you have more time to potter in the garden, then the cottage garden, edible garden, or herb garden may be better suited to your style.

5 Also consider the type of house you have and the garden style you prefer. You may like a more structured plan, or you may prefer a wilder garden. A more modern, airy feel is achieved with a meadow-style planting – the possibilities are endless.

Marking out beds and borders

When you have chosen a plan, and decided where it will fit in your garden, the next stage is to mark out the correct shape. As all plans are to the same scale of 1:50, measure the dimensions of the plan for your chosen bed or border and multiply these by 50. If you have a scale ruler the task is done for you, but an ordinary ruler is sufficient. You might find it easier to place a sheet of tracing paper over the plan and trace the outline first.

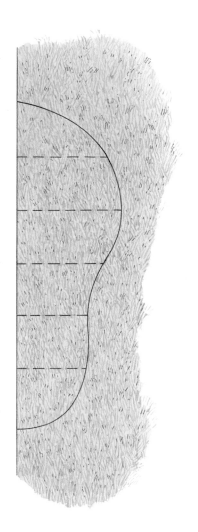

Marking out irregular-shaped borders

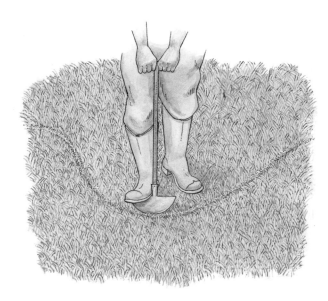

Using an edging iron

Irregular-shaped beds and borders

- Draw a straight line down the centre of the border on your tracing or, if it has one, use the straight line at the back. This will be the base line you will work from.

- Mark out the appropriate length in your garden using a garden line.

- To achieve the correct shape, draw lines at right angles at regular intervals along the base line to the edges of the border.

- Mark out corresponding lines in the garden, marking each point with a cane or stake.

- Use sand to join these points up and mark the outline of the border.

If you have marked out your border in existing turf, you now need to cut round the edge.

You can use a spade for this, or an edging iron for a neater edge. Stand upright and push whichever tool you are using vertically into the ground.

Regular-shaped beds and borders

To mark out borders based on squares or rectangles you need to achieve a right angle at each corner. This may be done by eye, but if you want to be really accurate you can use the 'right-angled triangle', or '3, 4, 5' method (see facing page).

- Mark out your first line.

- Place a stake or cane on the corner for your right angle (cane A).

- Fix a tape measure to the stake and measure 4m back from it, placing your second cane at B.

- Measure out another 5m from this and hold a cane at this point.

- Measure out a further 3m and meet up with cane A.

- Fix in cane C.

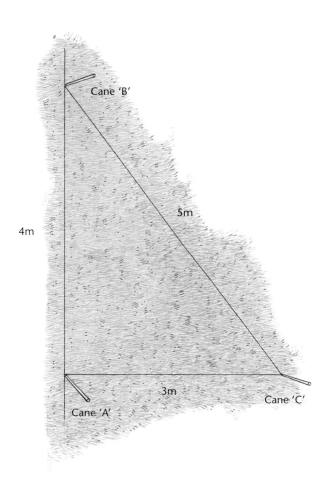

Cane 'B'

5m

4m

3m

Cane 'A'   Cane 'C'

'Right-angled triangle' method

It is the proportions of the triangle which achieve the right angle. 3, 4 and 5 metres (or 9, 12 and 15ft) are convenient measurements to use. If you have plenty of space you can use 6, 8 and 10 metres (or 18, 24 and 30ft).

Initial preparation

However good the plants you buy, your planting is, or the plans you use, you will not create a successful garden without spending adequate time preparing the ground. A bit of extra time spent at this stage will save hours of extra time in years to come and will give the plants the best start possible. If you have sufficient time it is a good idea to prepare the soil well in advance. An ideal would be to complete all initial operations several

weeks or, if practicable, a few months before planting to allow the soil to settle and the organic matter to start decomposing.

1   Clear the ground of any rubbish. This may not apply if you are working in an established garden, but many gardens both new and old have builders rubble and other rubbish to clear at the outset.

2   Clear away any weeds and unwanted plants. Take special care to rid the ground of troublesome perennial weeds such as couch grass or bindweed, digging deep to ensure all vestiges of the roots are removed.

3   Digging over the cleared area is the next important stage, and this is a good opportunity to thoroughly cultivate the ground and improve the soil by incorporating organic matter before planting (see 'Improving your soil', overleaf). Some plants are cleared away at the end of each season and new ones replanted every year, but many are going to be in place for years. Once your bed or border is established you will not be able to cultivate deeply around shrubs and trees, as root systems will be disturbed.

The technique of single digging is generally sufficient, i.e. digging to the depth of the spade, or one 'spit'. Use a spade for this initial cultivation and work methodically, digging out a trench and working backwards, to avoid treading on the soil you have dug. If the plot to be prepared divides neatly in two, work down one half, turn and work back up the other half. When you reach the end of the trench where the edge of the border is, turn this spadeful of soil in towards the centre of the bed. This will help to create a clear edge to your new border. Place the soil you have removed from the first trench close to your finishing line, to minimise the amount of soil that needs to be moved.

Keep the spade vertical as you cut sections of the soil. Lift the spade and turn the soil into the trench in front, inverting it completely. To avoid backache, work with manageable portions, do not attempt to turn over too much at a time, and straighten your back between each operation.

If the soil at the bottom of the trench is very compacted it is a good idea to break it up, to help it to drain better. Use a fork for this operation and break up the soil without mixing the top and bottom layers of soil.

Improving your soil

Organic matter is essential for a healthy soil. Different borders and plants may have different requirements, but a soil lacking in organic matter is lifeless and difficult to work. Organic matter can be incorporated while you are digging – an easy way to do this is to spread a layer of about 5–8cm (2–3in) of well-rotted manure or compost over the surface of the ground and then simply turn it into the trench as you dig. Another method is to place the organic matter in the trench as you work. This is probably the less messy method as you do not have to tread on the compost.

If you are digging in an area of existing turf, this turf can be used to improve the condition of the soil. This should only be done if the turf is free of troublesome perennial weeds and the

digging is carried out several months before planting. Cut off the turf in thin slices as you work, and invert it in the bottom of your trench. It is important to then chop up the turf well with your spade. If it is left whole it may cause problems with drainage as it can take a long time to decompose and will then form a barrier which impedes the flow of water through the soil. Once the turf has been chopped up, fill in the trench in the normal way.

There are many alternatives for supplying organic matter:

1 Farmyard manure (FYM) is a traditional source, and a useful way of adding organic matter in bulk. Depending on your locality it may be readily available, or an impractical option. If you can obtain a good supply you will also require the space to stack it before use. FYM should never be used fresh. Straw-based manures are preferable and will be ready in a few months. Those based on wood chips, shavings or sawdust may take a year or more to rot down. Stack the manure in a heap, water if dry, and cover with well-secured

polythene until it is ready for incorporating into the soil or mulching.

2 Proprietary brands of bagged composts are readily available from garden centres and DIY stores, and provide a more convenient method of supplying organic matter. Look for soil-improving or planting composts rather than seed or potting composts. They may be of well-rotted farmyard manure, composted bark or many other materials. All will help to improve the structure of your soil.

3 Green waste may be available from your local council. This is a good way of recycling organic waste, but you must make sure the material is disease-free and compost it well before use.

4 Mushroom compost is an option if locally available. It is already fairly well-rotted and is generally supplied bagged, so is relatively convenient. As it has a high lime content it should not be used for plants that require an acid soil.

5 Garden compost is perhaps the best and most ecologically sound method of providing a source of organic matter for your garden. It provides the perfect solution for disposing of garden and vegetable waste, while providing a supply of free compost for your garden. Many different composters are now available. Obviously, if you are starting from scratch in your garden you will need to import some organic matter for initial cultivations. Plastic bins are useful for smaller gardens, or you can buy or construct your own wooden boxes if you have a bit more room. The capacity of the box should be at least 1m³ (1cu yd).

Plastic bins are ideal for small gardens

Filling the compost heap

There are two basic methods of making compost – the hot and the cold method. In the hot method, suitable materials are collected together and then added in layers, but all at the same time, i.e. the bin is filled completely, all in one go. The heat raised will kill off the majority of weed seeds, pests and diseases and the heap will rot quickly and be ready for use in a few months. In the cold method, layers of material are added as they are ready, and therefore this is often the more convenient method. However, it will not kill off so many weeds and diseases, and may take a year or so to rot down. With both methods it is important to use a good mix of ingredients, to incorporate air into the heap, to keep it moist but not too wet, and to keep the heap covered.

Materials for adding to a compost heap:
- Vegetable peelings
- Animal manures (from vegetarian animals, e.g. horse, cow and domestic pets such as rabbits, guinea pigs)
- Straw
- Grass cuttings (in thin layers)
- Garden waste (annual weeds before they have seeded, soft stemmed prunings)
- Shredded woody prunings

Materials you must not add:
- Diseased plant material
- Perennial weeds such as couch grass
- Cooked vegetables or other food
- Woody material which has not been shredded

6 Leaf mould. If you have a good supply of autumn leaves it is best to compost them separately, rather than add them to the compost heap. An open, wire mesh container is suitable for making leaf mould. It generally takes a year or more before the leaf mould is ready for use.

Buying plants

Just as the creation of good soil conditions is important, so is the selection of healthy plants. Most plants are sold in containers nowadays. This gives much greater flexibility in planting times as you can plant throughout the year in suitable conditions.

When choosing plants avoid:
- Plants which are pot bound (roots may be seen coming out of the bottom of the pot)
- Plants with weeds growing in the pots
- Plants with any damage, pests or disease
- Weak and spindly growth
- Dried out compost
- Yellowing growth (unless this is a feature of the plant)

Some nurseries supply bare-rooted plants. These often establish themselves better and may be less expensive. However, they are only lifted at certain times of the year, and so there are restricted times for planting. For example, if you wanted to purchase a bare-rooted apple tree this would have to be between late autumn and early spring, the earlier the better. It is vital not to let bare-rooted plants dry out. If you obtain them before you are ready for planting, either leave them with the roots well wrapped in a frost-free shed or 'heel in' the plants. To do this, dig a temporary trench in the garden, lay the plants in at an angle and cover the roots with soil. Firm the soil around the roots to avoid frost damage.

Preparing soil for planting

After the initial digging, it is a good idea to leave the soil for a few weeks or months to allow the weather to break up the clods, and for the ground to settle. A heavy, clay soil will benefit in particular from being cultivated in the autumn and then being left rough over winter. Lighter soils are more adaptable in times of cultivation, as they will break up more easily.

Before you can start planting, the ground needs to be broken up to a finer tilth. Use a fork for this operation. The idea is to break up the top 10–12cm (4–5in) without turning over the soil again. Aim at roughly levelling the soil as you work. Finally, use a rake to break up any remaining clods and achieve a level surface.

If the bed or border you are preparing is set in turf, make sure you have a good, firm, clean edge. To achieve this you can tread the edges at an angle of 45° once the top is level (see

Heeling-in a bare-rooted tree

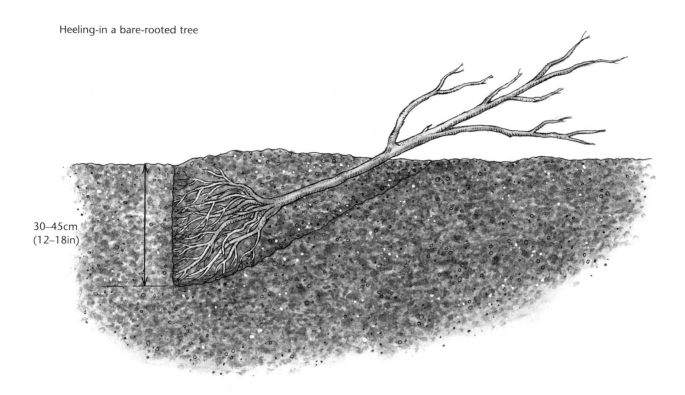

30–45cm
(12–18in)

illustration on right). Your border is now ready for planting. If you are going to sow seed rather than plant, you will need to firm the soil more, and this is explained in 'Sowing Outdoors', on page 12.

Planting

It is important to choose the right conditions for planting. Most container-grown plants may be planted at any time of the year in suitable conditions. The soil should not be too wet or too dry and planting should never be done in frosty weather. Also, avoid planting in very windy or very hot and dry conditions. However, perfect, text book conditions do not always exist and it is often a case of making the most of the conditions you are confronted with in the real world. If the soil is dry, water thoroughly before planting, checking that the water has penetrated deep into the soil. In extremes of temperature or windy weather, provide some temporary protection for the plants, e.g. horticultural fleece, shade netting or cloches.

Certain plants are best planted at particular times of the year, and some will only be available at specific times. If they are bare rooted they must be planted at these times:

Creating a firm edge

- Herbaceous perennials: autumn or spring
- Evergreen shrubs and conifers: early to mid-autumn or early to mid-spring
- Deciduous trees and shrubs: late autumn to early spring

A common mistake is to make the planting holes too small for the root balls of the plants. Dig a straight-sided hole which is deep and

Planting a small container-grown plant

wide enough for the size of the plant. Use a spade for larger plants, a trowel for small ones. Check the depth of the hole by placing the plant in it – the plant should sit at the same depth as it was in the container or nursery. For bare-rooted plants the soil mark can generally be seen on the stem.

It is vital that the plants have not dried out at the time of planting. If they are dry, soak bare-rooted plants in a bucket of water, or water any container-grown plants a few hours before planting. Remove container-grown plants carefully from their pots, without damaging the stems and, if necessary, gently tease out any spiralling roots. Position the plant in the prepared hole and gradually fill in with topsoil or a planting mix: equal parts of topsoil and composted bark with a handful of bonemeal, or a proprietary brand of planting compost. Make sure there are no air pockets left, firm the plant well and water in.

Sowing

Nurseries and garden centres stock a wide range of plants, and the advent of 'plug' plants makes growing on and transplanting very much easier. However, many plants are easily raised from seed at home, without the need for any expensive equipment and, if you do have the time to raise your own plants, it is very satisfying and extends your choice of plants.

Sowing outdoors

For sowing outdoors, the soil needs to be warm and moist – neither too wet nor too dry – and you must prepare a good, firm seedbed. Prepare the soil as for planting (see page 11), breaking up the soil to a fine tilth, then tread the soil to firm it. Walk up and down methodically, to cover the area to be prepared. Rake over the soil again, to achieve a level surface with fine particles of soil.

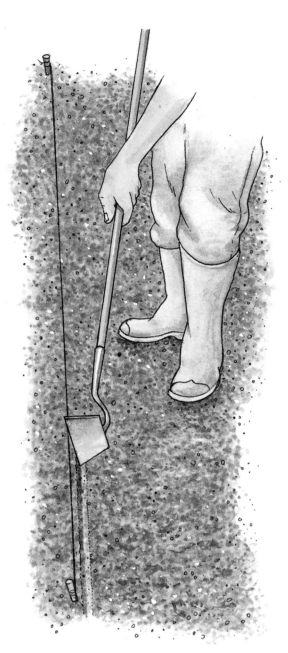

There are two basic methods of sowing seeds: either broadcasting or sowing in drills. Broadcasting is a useful method for awkward areas and seed that does not have to be sown too deeply. Scatter the seed thinly and evenly over the prepared area and gently rake in.

Sowing in drills ensures the seeds are well covered and will enable you to distinguish the seedlings more easily as they germinate. If you mark the rows, it is easier to hoe between them to control any germinating weed seedlings.

Fix a garden line where you want to sow your seed, making sure it is taut and secure. Using the edge of a draw hoe or the back of a rake, draw or mark out a v-shaped drill to a depth of about 1cm (½in) for small seeds, deeper for larger seeds. Scatter seed thinly and evenly along the drill and gently rake back the soil to cover the seeds.

Seeds may also be sown in 'stations' along the seed drills. Three or four seeds are sown at intervals along the drill. By spacing them at the correct spacing required for the mature plants, you will cut down on the need for subsequent thinning. It is a good idea to cover the area with netting or twiggy sticks to prevent pets and birds disturbing the seedbed.

Making a seed drill

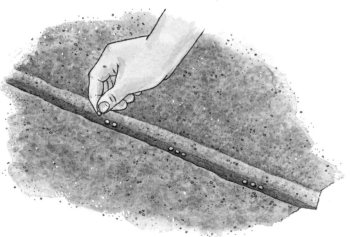

Sowing seed in 'stations'

When the seedlings are large enough to distinguish from any weed seedlings, thin them to the required spacing by selecting the strongest seedlings you wish to retain, and gently pulling out the unwanted ones, along with any weeds. For the station-sown seedlings, simply thin to one seedling per station.

Hardy annuals

Hardy annuals are particularly suitable for raising from seed and may be sown where they are to flower. Annuals are those plants which complete their life cycles within a year, i.e. they germinate, flower, produce seed and die in the one growing season. Hardy annuals are those annuals which can withstand colder conditions, and are therefore very often sown outdoors. They do, however, require relatively warm temperatures to germinate and most are best sown outdoors in early to mid-spring in suitable conditions.

Biennials

As the name implies, biennials complete their life cycle within two years. They normally produce leafy growth in the first year, overwinter and then flower the following year. Many plants, such as sweet Williams (*Dianthus barbatus*), are traditionally grown as biennials although they will live for longer. Sow biennials outdoors in late spring/early summer, preferably in a separate nursery bed. Water the rows of plants well before lifting them in the autumn for transplanting to their final positions.

Alternatively, these can be raised in a greenhouse (see 'Herbaceous perennials' below). Seed trays or modules may be used for pricking out the seedlings.

Herbaceous perennials

Perennials are those plants which will live for longer than two years. Some may have very long life cycles. Herbaceous perennials have a top growth which is soft and often dies back over the winter months.

They vary in their ease of growing successfully from seed but some – e.g. *Echinacea purpurea*, *Rudbeckia* 'Goldsturm' and *Achillea millefolium* – are particularly suitable. Some of the planting plans have fairly large numbers of herbaceous perennials planted together in drifts for greater effect. Raising

these from seed provides a less expensive option for obtaining sufficient numbers of plants.

The easiest method is probably to raise these in pots indoors, preferably in a greenhouse. Sowing times vary, but spring or autumn are generally suitable. Fill a small plastic pot with seed compost, gently firm and level the compost and sow seed thinly on the surface. Cover with a fine layer of sieved seed compost, label and water in. Once the seedlings are large enough to handle they should be pricked out. Fill the required number of individual pots with potting compost and gently firm. Then, using a small dibber or pencil, gently lever out the seedlings without damaging them. Select the strongest and handle them by their seed leaves, not the stems which will easily break. Make a hole in the centre of the compost, deep enough to take the delicate roots. Lower the seedling in, gently firm and water in. Grow the plants on in a greenhouse or cold frame and then harden them off before planting them out. To harden off, gradually acclimatize the plants to colder temperatures – by allowing more ventilation, or standing them outdoors – for increasing periods of time.

Aftercare

Weeding

Weeds compete with your plants for moisture, space and nutrients, and may also harbour pests and diseases. A weed may be defined as a plant growing where it is not wanted, and so what is considered a weed in one garden, may be welcomed in another. There are, however, many weeds which most people would want to keep under control and, even in a wildlife garden, careful control is necessary to keep the desired balance of plants. Methods to control weeds include simple hand weeding using a border fork, or hand fork amongst smaller, more delicate plants, and hoeing which may be useful for larger areas.

Weed control matting is another option. This should be placed over the soil once it has been prepared for planting, and the edges should be buried to secure it firmly. Cut cross-shaped slits to plant through, then top with a decorative mulch, such as bark chippings, to make it look more attractive. Although this is very labour saving, it is not appropriate for plants which require regular feeding or mulching, such as newly planted trees.

Mulching

This is another excellent method for controlling weeds, as long as the mulch itself is weed-free. It will also help improve the condition of the soil and may provide plant nutrients. Another benefit of some types of mulch is that it will help the soil to warm up quickly. Various materials can be used according to availability, type of plants and situation. These include well-rotted farmyard manure, garden compost, leaf mould, bark chippings and gravel or stone chippings.

Watering

By choosing the right plan for your situation, the need for watering should be kept at a minimum. However, if conditions are particularly dry, especially in the first year or so after planting, it may be necessary to water. Give the plants a thorough soaking to ensure the water penetrates well and, if possible, water in the evening to avoid losses by evaporation. Take particular care that any young seedlings do not dry out, and water them with a fine spray in dry conditions.

Pruning

Individual requirements of different plants are discussed in the appropriate chapters, but these general principles should be followed:

- Make sure your tools, e.g. secateurs, are sharp and clean
- Always cut out any dead, damaged or diseased material

Deadheading, staking and training

These are covered under individual chapters. Deadheading is important for some plants to keep the continuity of flowering. Some of the taller-flowered perennials require staking and wall-grown shrubs and climbers will need training.

Pests and diseases

'Prevention is better than cure' is a good adage for dealing with the problem of pests and diseases in the garden and, by choosing the correct plants for your situation, you are taking the first step in avoiding trouble. Providing your plants with a well-prepared soil and good growing conditions is the second. A healthy, strong-growing plant is far less likely to succumb to pests and disease than a weak one.

A question of balance is important in the garden. Learn to recognise beneficial insects and encourage them and other predators into your garden. Birds may cause problems at some times of the year in the garden, but they will consume vast quantities of insects and grubs throughout their lifetimes. Hedgehogs, frogs and toads are invaluable at keeping down numbers of slugs. Both ladybirds and their larvae are excellent at aphid control, likewise the hoverfly and lacewing.

However, even in the best gardens problems occur. To avoid the spread of any disease always keep a look out for any dead, damaged or diseased material. Cut this out straight away and dispose of it (in the dustbin, or by burning if practicable). Always use tools that are clean and sharp and avoid any damage to plants during cultivation.

Part Two

The Planting Plans

Spring Garden

Selected plants:

1. *Osmanthus delavayi*
2. *Chaenomeles × superba* 'Crimson and Gold' (flowering quince)
3. *Viburnum × juddii* (viburnum)
4. *Viburnum carlesii* (viburnum)
5. *Mahonia aquifolium* (Oregon grape)
6. *Amelanchier lamarckii* (Juneberry)
7. *Geranium macrorrhizum* 'Ingwersen's Variety' x 8
8. *Bergenia* 'Abendglut' x 3
9. *Euphorbia polychroma* x 3 (milkweed/spurge)
10. *Bergenia* 'Silberlicht' x 3
11. *Crocus tommasinianus* (crocus)
12. *Hyacinthoides hispanica* (Spanish bluebell)
13. *Narcissus* 'February Gold' (daffodil)

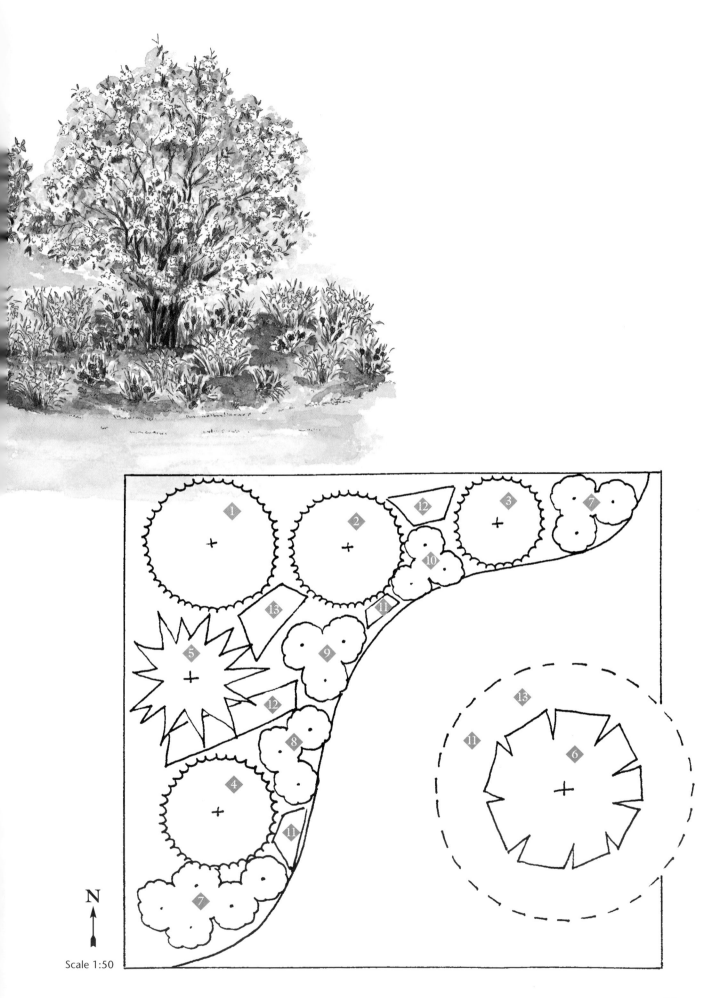

N

Scale 1:50

Spring Garden

Spring flowers are always a welcome sight. This garden brings a sequence of colour from early to late spring, with a mixture of bulbs, shrubs and perennials. A sweeping lawn path leads you between the scents and colours of the corner border, and the circle of naturalized bulbs.

A basic framework of five shrubs – the osmanthus, chaenomeles, two viburnums and mahonia – provides structure throughout the year in the corner border. This is balanced by the larger form of the specimen shrub *Amelanchier lamarckii* which is planted in the lawn. The same cultivars of daffodils (*Narcissus* 'February Gold') and species of crocuses (*Crocus tommasinianus*) are planted in the border and naturalized in the grass, bringing a sense of unity to the planting scheme.

Amelanchier lamarckii (Juneberry)

Site

The plants chosen will grow in any reasonable soil, but will thrive best in a site which has well-drained but moisture-retentive soil. The osmanthus will benefit from a protected south-facing aspect, while a well-drained soil will be particularly beneficial to the bulbs.

Plants and planting

Set out the five shrubs in the border and plant these first of all. Two are evergreens with glossy, yet contrasting foliage: *Osmanthus delavayi* has smaller dark green leaves and a round shape, and produces a profusion of scented, tubular, white flowers from mid- to late spring. *Mahonia aquifolium* brings a contrast with spiny foliage. Attractive red tints often appear in the leaves, particularly when grown in poorer soils. This creates a wonderful effect against the scented, deep yellow flowers in early to mid-spring.

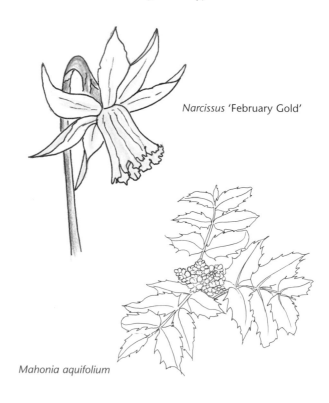

Narcissus 'February Gold'

Mahonia aquifolium

Crocus tommasinianus

Chaenomeles × superba **'Crimson and Gold'**

Chaenomeles × superba 'Crimson and Gold' is a hybrid of the 'flowering quinces' or 'japonicas' which is easier to look after than the straightforward species. They form neat, rounded shrubs without the need for much pruning. 'Crimson and Gold' is a vibrant choice with golden anthers displayed against the crimson petals. As a bonus it also produces golden yellow fruits in the autumn which may be used for jelly making.

Viburnum carlesii and *Viburnum × juddii* both flower later in the spring. *V. carlesii* has pink-budded white flowers, while those of *V. × juddii* open to a pale pink. The foliage is soft and downy, contrasting with the glossy evergreen foliage. These shrubs also colour well in the autumn with red tints.

Next you can plant the groups of perennials. I've started with bergenias, which have the common name of 'elephant's ears', an apt description of their large leathery leaves. *Bergenia* 'Abendglut' has rich, maroon-tinted leaves with dark, purple-red, semi-double flowers in mid-spring; these contrast with the silver-white flowers of *Bergenia* 'Silberlicht', which tinge with pink as they age.

Geranium macrorrhizum 'Ingwersen's Variety' carries the flowering interest on into late spring. The aromatic, lobed leaves are lighter in both colour and texture than the bergenias and soft pink flowers are produced from late spring onwards. The foliage also colours well in the autumn with scarlet and russet tints.

Bergenia **'Abendglut'**

Euphorbia polychroma

Euphorbia polychroma is a bushy perennial which has mounds of sulphur-yellow flowers in mid- to late spring. It looks effective planted against other strong colours such as crimsons and golds of the mahonia, bergenias and chaenomeles.

Specimen shrub

Amelanchier lamarckii can be a small tree or large shrub (see p. 20). The young coppery foliage starts to unfurl early in spring and is shortly followed by masses of star-shaped white flowers from mid to late spring. In autumn the brilliant red and orange leaves make a spectacular display.

To plant this in the lawn:

* Position the amelanchier as shown in the plan, approximately 3m (10ft) from the nearest edge of the border

* Mark a 1m (3ft) diameter circle in the lawn around the amelanchier

* Cut the turf away from the circle

* Prepare the soil for planting
This area should be kept free of grass and weeds to enable the tree to establish, and for mulching and feeding.

Bulbs and corms

Daffodils may be planted from late summer to mid-autumn, but the earlier you can plant them the better. The bulbs should be planted 10–15cm (4–6in) deep and a similar distance apart. To achieve a natural effect, scatter the bulbs by hand and then adjust spacing so that the bulbs do not touch.

The one used here is *Narcissus* 'February Gold' (see p. 20), an early daffodil with cheery, bright yellow flowers and slightly reflexed petals. This is a medium-sized daffodil, which will withstand wind damage better than some of the taller top-heavy cultivars.

Crocus tommasinianus is an early crocus with funnel-shaped, purple flowers which open wide in the sunlight (see p. 21). Plant these crocus corms from early to late autumn at a depth of 7.5cm (3in) and a distance of 10cm (4in) apart.

Hyacinthoides hispanica (Spanish bluebell) requires similar spacing and depth of planting (see photograph on facing page). You must be careful not to let the bulbs dry out, so these should be planted as soon as they are available, usually from late summer to early autumn. Strap-shaped glossy leaves appear early in spring, followed by spires of blue, and sometimes pink or white, bell-shaped flowers. These carry the flowering interest through to late spring.

Naturalizing bulbs in grass

The bulbs chosen for the border will all naturalize well in grass.

1 First of all cut the grass

2 Mark out the circle to contain the planted bulbs

3 Plant in drifts of the same flowers, scattering the bulbs to achieve a more natural effect

4 Use a trowel or special bulb planter for the daffodils

5 Remove a core of soil and place a little grit or coarse sand and bonemeal in the bottom of the hole

6 Gently firm the bulb in, the correct way up, fattest end down

7 Break up the core of soil and replace it around the bulb, making sure there are no air pockets

For the smaller crocus corms and bluebell bulbs it is easier to lift sections of turf. Lightly fork the soil underneath, incorporating coarse sand or grit and a little bonemeal. Scatter the corms or bulbs and gently firm into the soil before replacing and firming the turf.

Hyacinthoides hispanica (**Spanish bluebell**)

It is important to allow the foliage of the bulbs to die back naturally, both in the border and the grass. The food produced in the leaves is passed back into the bulb or corm to provide food for next year's flowers and foliage. The grass should not be cut until at least six weeks after the flowers have faded and, if possible, leave until the leaves have died back completely. Deadhead the flower stems by cutting back below the seed head, so that energy will go back into the bulb rather than being used for seed production.

Once established, this spring garden will be relatively easy to look after. The shrubs require minimal pruning, the perennials are low maintenance and the bulbs will spread naturally to carpet the border and circle of lawn.

Other spring-flowering shrubs

Ribes sanguineum (flowering currant)
Forsythia × *intermedia*
Berberis darwinii (Darwin's barberry)
Kerria japonica
Spiraea 'Arguta' (bridal wreath)
Magnolia stellata (star magnolia)

Selected plants:

1. *Rosa* Glamis Castle x 3
2. *Rosa* Claire Rose® x 3
3. *Rosa* The Dark Lady x 3
4. *Catananche caerulea* x 9

5. *Dianthus* 'Doris' x 4 (modern pink)
6. *Dianthus* 'Mrs Sinkins' x 4 (old-fashioned pink)
7. *Dianthus* 'Gran's Favourite' x 4 (old-fashioned pink)
8. *Salvia farinacea* 'Victoria' (sage)

Circular
Summer Bed

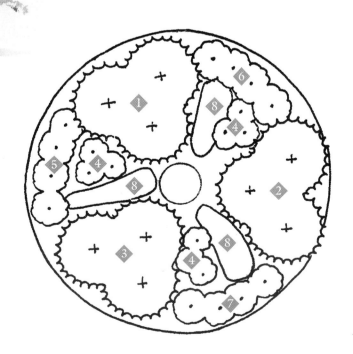

N

Scale 1:50

Circular Summer Bed

Choose a site which is sheltered from strong winds, but fairly open and sunny, and place a sundial or ornament of your choice to give a central focal point.

Mark out a circle as described in the Herb Garden (page 84), but to a radius of 2m (6ft 6in). Dig over the bed, removing any weeds and incorporating well-rotted manure or compost. If planting on ground which has grown roses before, the soil must be dug out and replaced, otherwise the new roses will not thrive.

Plants and planting

Three groups of roses, also planted in threes for greater effect, will give a scented display of white, pink and deep red flowers. Those chosen are English roses, which combine old-fashioned charm with the modern attributes of repeat flowering. However, a range of this type of cultivar is becoming increasingly available and, as there is plenty of choice, use those I have selected as a guideline only:

Rosa Dark Lady is a deep red, velvet-textured rose on slightly arching stems.

R. Claire Rose® is a pale pink and *R.* Glamis Castle a pure white.

Cottage garden pinks provide an edging between the groups of roses, with their blue-green foliage and scented summer flowers. *Dianthus* 'Doris' is a modern pink with pink flowers and a deeper centre. *D.* 'Gran's Favourite' is an old-fashioned, very fragrant pink with white petals and deep pink-maroon edging and centres. *D.* 'Mrs Sinkins' is an old-fashioned fragrant pink, with white frilly petals. As with the roses, I suggest you use this selection as a guide, as there is a vast range of attractive garden pinks available.

Rosa **Glamis Castle**

Dianthus 'Doris'

Roses and salvias

Plant long drifts of the upright *Salvia farinacea* 'Victoria', to contrast with the rounded shapes of the roses. The flowers are a purple-blue and are held on tall purple-blue square-sided stems, lasting well into the autumn. They are perennials but are not hardy, so need to be purchased or raised from seed each year. Sow in gentle heat in early spring and harden off before planting out in late spring/early summer. Space plants about 30cm (12in) apart.

Another plant to add a touch of blue is *Catananche caerulea*. This is a perennial, with wiry stems and cornflower-like flowers.

Aftercare

The roses will require regular pruning every spring. Firstly, cut out any dead, diseased, damaged or weak material. Then cut back remaining healthy shoots – by about half to one third of their length – to outward facing buds. After pruning, apply a mulch of well-rotted manure or compost.

Catananche caerulea

29

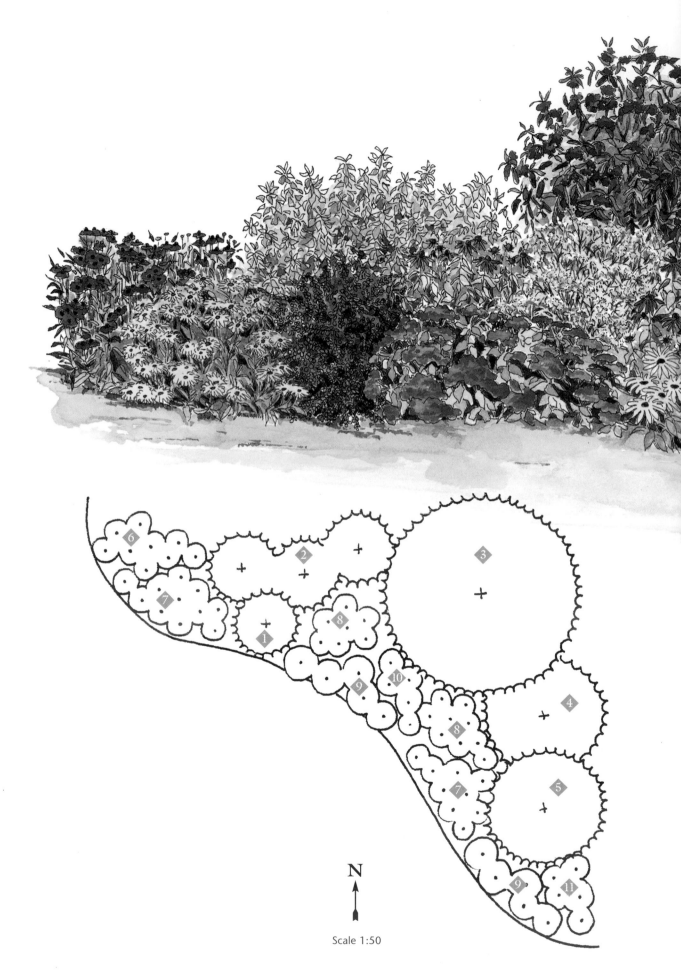

N

Scale 1:50

Autumn Border

Selected plants:

1. *Berberis thunbergii* 'Golden Ring'
2. *Euonymus japonicus* 'Ovatus Aureus' x 3
3. *Cotoneaster* 'Cornubia'
4. *Kerria japonica* 'Pleniflora'
5. *Cotinus* 'Flame' (smoke bush)
6. *Helenium* 'Moerheim Beauty' x 9
7. *Rudbeckia* 'Goldsturm' x 20 (coneflower)
8. *Echinacea purpurea* x 16 (purple coneflower)
9. *Sedum* 'Herbstfreude' x 10
10. *Aster turbinellus* x 5
11. *Helenium* 'Butterpat' x 5

Autumn Border

People tend to regard autumn as the time for cutting back and tidying away at the end of the year. Many plants, however, come into their own in this season. Some produce colourful berries, others continue or come into flower. The spectacular autumn leaf colour of many trees is well known and admired. Many smaller shrubs also complete the season with displays of brilliant reds and yellows. Being much smaller, they have the advantage of providing the display without the vast quantities of leaves to clear as they fall.

This autumn border includes a range of autumn flowering perennials, and shrubs for berries and leaf colour. It is suitable for most soils, apart from extremes of acid or chalky soils, and will benefit from a sunny position. The latter will both produce and display the best autumn colours.

Shrubs

After thorough preparation, plant the framework of shrubs first. Start with the impressive cornerstone of *Cotoneaster* 'Cornubia'. This is a large, tall-growing, evergreen/semi-evergreen shrub which produces an abundance of large red fruits on arching branches. The cotoneasters are a very useful genus of plants for autumn interest, and this particular one has some of the largest berries.

Euonymus japonicus 'Ovatus Aureus' is an evergreen which provides all-year interest, its emerald foliage variegated with deep yellow. Plant it in the autumn border as a bright backdrop to display the low-arching stems of fiery red foliage of the berberis.

Berberis thunbergii 'Golden Ring' is an attractive shrub throughout the summer, and the name refers to the golden edging of the purple foliage. The entire leaf then develops rich red autumn colouring.

Cotinus

Kerria japonica 'Pleniflora' has tall, straight stems and spreads quickly by suckering. It is usually only planted with the orange spring flowers in mind, but it comes into its own again in the autumn, when the mid-green foliage turns to golden yellow. Kerria provides a contrast both in colour and form when planted by the rounded smoke bush.

Cotinus 'Flame' (smoke bush) gives an airy display of feathery plumes of pinkish flowers in the summer, and these are followed by brilliant scarlet-red autumn tints (see photograph above).

Herbaceous perennials

For the greatest impact, plant these perennials in bold drifts. Either purchase container-grown plants, or, if you are prepared to wait a little longer, raise from seed. Several of the perennials, such as rudbeckias and echinaceas are easily grown from seed, and many will even flower in their first season.

Helenium 'Moerheim Beauty' has bronze-red, daisy like flowers. *H.* 'Butterpat', as the name implies, is a golden yellow. They both flower from late summer into the autumn. Regular division in the spring or autumn will be beneficial.

Echinacea purpurea (purple coneflower) has a very attractive flower shape. The prominent cone- shaped central disc is surrounded by strongly reflexed purple petals, or strictly speaking, ray florets.

Rudbeckia 'Goldsturm' (coneflower) also has striking flowers, bright yellow contrasting with the black central disc.

Aster turbinellus has wiry stems topped with a haze of mauve daisy flowers. This aster has the advantage of being resistant to mildew, which can be unsightly in other species.

Sedum 'Herbstfreude' has large, flat heads of flowers, which turn from deep pink to russet-brown and form horizontal layers, which contrast with the upright stems of all the daisy family perennials. Leave these sedum flower heads on through autumn into winter for an attractive display.

Helenium **'Moerheim Beauty'**

Aftercare

The border will benefit from a thick, organic mulch applied every spring.

The shrubs require little regular pruning, apart from the kerria – when this has finished flowering (around early summer) cut back the old shoots which have flowered to ground level.

Leave the attractive seedheads on these herbaceous perennials and then cut them back to ground level in the spring.

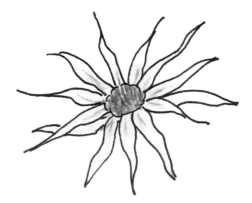

Rudbeckia 'Goldsturm'

Sedum 'Herbstfreude'

Plants selected:

 *Viburnum tinus* 'Eve Price'

 *Viburnum × bodnantense* 'Dawn'

 *Garrya elliptica* 'James Roof'

 *Lonicera fragrantissima* (shrubby honeysuckle)

 *Mahonia × media* 'Charity'

 *Cornus sanguinea* 'Midwinter Fire' x 3 (dogwood)

 *Phormium* 'Sundowner'

 *Helleborus argutifolius* x 6 (Corsican hellebore)

 *Helleborus orientalis* x 8

 *Iris foetidissima* (stinking iris)

 *Galanthus nivalis* (common snowdrop)

Winter Garden

Bird
Table

3

8

4

8

5

9

9

11

2

6

1

7

10

N

Scale 1:50

Winter Garden

A cheering garden is more important than ever in the depths of winter. Make sure that winter-interest plants are situated close to the house, near windows or pathways, so they can be enjoyed to the full.

This garden is based on a courtyard design, ideally adjoining a house with patio doors or windows overlooking the garden, so that the plants can be viewed from the warmth of indoors. It could be a garden in itself, bounded by walls or fencing, or a garden room within a larger garden, separated by paths, lawn, trellis or hedging. Beech hedging with its russet-brown foliage over winter would make a wonderful backdrop.

The central part of the courtyard could be paving or gravel, for easy access and low maintenance. Alternatively, it could be lawn with stepping stones to reach the centrally placed bird table.

Plants and planting

This garden includes a mixture of deciduous and evergreen shrubs and perennials and will require relatively little maintenance once established. Many of the winter-flowering shrubs are highly scented and have very long flowering periods, while other shrubs have different attractions in winter such as catkins or brightly coloured stems.

Garrya elliptica 'James Roof' is an evergreen with wavy edged, dark green foliage. The long

Garrya elliptica

Glowing stems of *Cornus sanguinea* **'Midwinter Fire'**

catkins, produced in abundance throughout the winter, are its particular attraction. The male cultivars of *Garrya elliptica*, of which this is a popular example, have more spectacular catkins.

Mahonia × media 'Charity' has glossy, spiky foliage and a bold upright form. In the winter, this is topped by bright yellow spikes of scented flowers.

Between these two evergreens, plant the deciduous *Lonicera fragrantissima*. This is a spreading, bushy honeysuckle which flowers on bare stems in the winter. The flowers are creamy white and delicate, with a sweet, pervasive scent.

Viburnum × bodnantense 'Dawn' is another deciduous shrub which has scented flowers. The deep pink flower buds open to paler pink flowers on upright, bare stems, contrasting well with *Viburnum tinus* 'Eve Price' which is evergreen, and has a rounded form. With flattish heads of rose budded, pink-white flowers produced for months on end, this must be one of the longest flowering shrubs. Further interest is added by the reddish stems and blue-black fruits.

The above shrubs require little regular pruning, apart from *Lonicera fragrantissima* which will benefit from annual pruning after flowering. Cut back those shoots which have flowered to strong new growths.

A group of dogwoods are included for their winter stems. *Cornus sanguinea* 'Midwinter Fire' has particularly bright stems. The name is so apt,

Helleborus orientalis

Selected plants:

1. *Hedera helix* 'Parsley Crested' (ivy)
2. *Jasminum nudiflorum* (winter jasmine)
3. *Pyracantha* 'Orange Glow'
4. *Cotoneaster salicifolius* 'Pendulus'
5. *Euonymus fortunei* 'Silver Queen'
6. *Ribes laurifolium*
7. *Euonymus japonicus* 'Ovatus Aureus' x 3
8. *Kerria japonica* 'Pleniflora'
9. *Pulmonaria saccharata* x 5
10. *Heuchera* 'Palace Purple' x 5
11. *Polemonium caeruleum* x 5 (Jacob's ladder)
12. *Heuchera* 'Scintillation' x 5
13. *Anemone × hybrida* x 6

North-facing Border

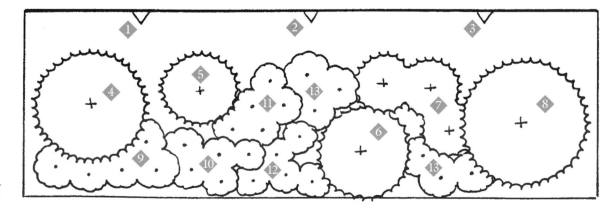

North-facing Border

This border is designed to back onto a north-facing wall or fence. The protection provided by a wall or fence provides an opportunity to grow a range of climbers, but plants need to be selected with care. I have included a selection of climbers, shrubs and perennials to give height, variety and seasonal interest.

Support for climbers

It is best to fix some supports to the wall or fence before preparing the border, to avoid trampling over the newly dug soil. Ivies are self-clinging, but may need some encouragement to grow in the right direction. Jasmines can be displayed more effectively if they have support, while pyracanthas can be grown as freestanding bushes, but will also give a good display if trained against a wall or fence.

Starting at 30cm (12in) from the ground, fix galvanized vine eyes or screw eyes 1.5–2m (5ft–6ft 6in) apart. If fixing to a fence, use the spacing of the fence posts. Carry on at 50cm (20in) intervals and stretch 10–14 gauge galvanized wire horizontally between the vine eyes. To achieve a really taut wire, use a special straining bolt at one end.

Once the wires are in place the ground can be dug over, with the addition of organic matter.

Plants and planting

Climbers/wall shrubs
Climbers should be planted at least 23cm (9in) from the wall or fence and inclined towards the support. If planted too close, particularly to a wall, the plants are likely to suffer from dry soil

Fixing wire support

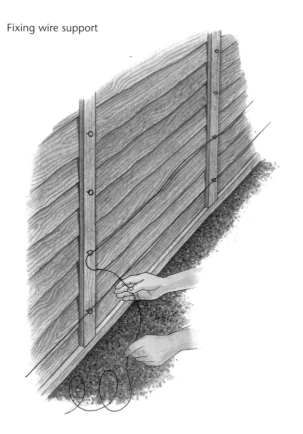

Hedera helix 'Parsley Crested'

Kerria japonica 'Pleniflora'

conditions. Dig a hole wide and deep enough to accommodate the roots and place some planting compost in the bottom. Check that the depth is correct and place the plant in, leaning it towards the wall or fence. If the nursery has provided a cane, leave it in – it can be removed later, once the plant is established in the required direction of growth.

The evergreen *Hedera helix* 'Parsley Crested' is an attractive ivy, with frilly-edged foliage (see illustration on facing page).

Pyracantha 'Orange Glow' is another evergreen, which has cream-white flowers followed by an autumn display of bright orange berries, which often last right through the winter. These berries are particularly enjoyed by blackbirds, and provide a valuable food source for them in harsh winters. In between the two evergreens, the deciduous *Jasminum nudiflorum* (winter jasmine) provides a cheerful centrepiece over the winter months, with bright yellow, starry flowers on arching green stems.

Shrubs

Cotoneaster salicifolius 'Pendulus' has narrow green leaves on weeping stems, and white summer flowers followed by red fruits. Buy it as a standard, if possible, as this will add immediate height and give the border some structure.

Dig a hole wide enough to take the roots of the plant comfortably, and deep enough to position

the plant at the same depth as it was planted previously. It will need a stake – positioned to be just to the back of the shrub – which must be put in before planting to avoid damaging the roots. Choose a stake that can be driven a minimum of 45cm (18in) into the ground, yet will still reach just below the head of the branches once the

Euonymus fortunei 'Silver Queen'

Selected plants:

1. *Perovskia atriplicifolia* 'Blue Spire' x 3 (Russian sage)
2. *Cistus × cyprius*
3. *Convolvulus cneorum* x 3
4. *Caryopteris × clandonensis* 'Heavenly Blue' x 3
5. *Phlomis fruticosa* (Jerusalem sage)
6. *Helianthemum* 'Wisley Primrose' x 3
7. *Helianthemum* 'Wisley Pink' x 3
8. *Phlomis italica*
9. *Cistus × corbariensis*
10. *Lotus hirsutus*
11. *Salvia officinalis* 'Purpurascens'
12. *Artemesia* 'Powis Castle' x 3
13. *Brachyglottis* 'Sunshine' (syn. *Senecio* 'Sunshine')
14. *Stipa gigantea* (giant oats)
15. *Pennisetum villosum* x 3 (feather-top)
16. *Sedum* 'Herbstfreude' x 2
17. *Catananche caerulea* x 5
18. *Festuca glauca* x 13 (blue fescue)

South-facing Border

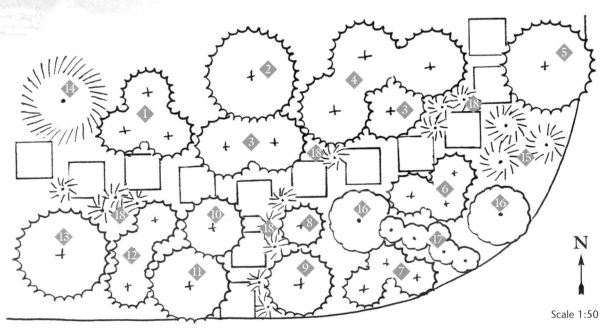

N

Scale 1:50

South-facing Border

I have chosen a selection of drought-resistant shrubs, perennials and grasses for this border. Many are low growing, so I've included a stepping-stone path for easy access, which enables you to wander through and enjoy all of the plants without having to arrange them in strict tiers. It makes cultivation easier, too, as everything is within easy reach.

The quality of drought-resistance in plants is increasingly important and many plants have adapted naturally to cope with hot and dry conditions, developing features that help the plant to reduce the amount of water it loses by evaporation from its leaves. So, if you are choosing plants for a sunny position, and do not want to be watering continuously, these are some features you could look out for:

- Silver-grey foliage
- Succulent leaves
- Narrow, rolled leaves
- Thick, leathery leaves
- Hairy leaves

Site and soil

This border is for a sunny position and a free-draining soil. As always, good preparation is important, with the addition of organic matter. However, the soil does not want to be too rich and you should avoid the use of any fresh, over-rich manures, as these could result in a lot of lush leafy growth which would not withstand dry conditions so well.

After preparing the soil, level and firm the area for the stepping stones. Set the stones out to provide access to the whole border, and walk along the path before setting the stones in firmly, to make sure the spacing suits a gentle walking stride. Once the stones are in place and the border is planted, you need rarely tread on the soil again which will benefit the soil structure.

Plants and planting

Hazy blue spires of *Perovskia atriplicifolia* 'Blue Spire' (Russian sage) and *Caryopteris × clandonensis* 'Heavenly Blue' form a soft backdrop for the border. These require little attention apart from cutting back in the spring.

The rounded evergreen form of *Cistus × cyprius* makes a centrepiece. The flowers of cistus only last a day each, but are produced in such profusion that they cover the shrubs in early summer. *Cistus × cyprius* has attractive papery, white flowers with crimson markings and a yellow centre. *Convolvulus cneorum* has white, funnel-shaped flowers and silver foliage which contrasts well with the dark green foliage of the cistus, while *Cistus × corbariensis* is lower growing, with white flowers and yellow centres, and buds which are an attractive pinkish-red.

Cistus × cyprius

Perovskia atriplicifolia

Euonymus fortunei 'Silver Queen'

Choisya 'Aztec Pearl'

cap flowers in early summer have deep pink centres surrounded by white, and are followed by red, autumn berries.

Sambucus racemosa 'Plumosa Aurea' is an elder which also has very attractive foliage, being finely cut and a bright gold; the frothy white flowers in early spring are followed by red berries.

Smaller shrubs are planted to the front of the border, with two groups of three *Potentilla fruticosa* at each end. These are deciduous shrubs with a very long flowering season, from late spring through to the autumn and in winter they have an attractive, dense and twiggy brown framework. The gentle, pale yellow flowers of *P. fruticosa* 'Primrose Beauty' blend with the silver of *Euonymus fortunei* 'Silver Queen'. The latter shrubs provide all-year interest with evergreen, variegated foliage and in winter the leaves are often tinged with pink.

The bright yellow flowers of *Potentilla fruticosa* 'Goldfinger' follow the yellow theme through from the foliage of both the elder and elaeagnus.

Choisya 'Aztec Pearl'

Choisya 'Aztec Pearl' has glossy, aromatic, evergreen foliage and clusters of scented white flowers, flushed with pink in late spring and summer. A group of three *Berberis thunbergii* f. *atropurpurea* bring purple foliage into the scheme, contrasting with the greens and yellows. They are spring flowering with pale yellow, red-tinged flowers, followed by red fruits and vivid red tints in the autumn.

Aftercare

No routine pruning is required apart from the cutting out of any dead, damaged or diseased material, as mentioned earlier. If you are using a weed-suppressant membrane, top up its decorative mulch covering as required. Otherwise, mulch after planting with a thick layer of well-rotted manure, compost or bark chippings and replenish this every spring.

Other low-maintenance shrubs

Aucuba japonica
Cotinus coggygria (smoke bush)
Cotoneaster
Elaeagnus pungens 'Maculata'
Hibiscus
Ligustrum ovalifolium 'Aureum'
Mahonia
Olearia (daisy bush)
Photinia davidiana
Prunus laurocerasus 'Otto Luyken'
Viburnum davidii
Viburnum rhytidophyllum

Selected plants:

1. *Cotoneaster salicifolius* 'Rothschildianus'
2. *Mahonia japonica*
3. *Mahonia aquifolium* 'Atropurpurea'
4. *Spiraea* 'Arguta' (bridal wreath)
5. *Mahonia × media* 'Winter Sun'
6. *Weigela* 'Bristol Ruby'
7. *Abelia × grandiflora*
8. *Spiraea japonica* 'Goldflame' x 3
9. *Spiraea thunbergii*
10. *Ceratostigma willmottianum* x 8
11. *Sarcococca confusa*
12. *Deutzia × rosea* x 3
13. *Abelia* Confetti x 3

Shrub Bed with All-year Interest

N

Scale 1:50

Selected plants:

1. *Buddleja davidii* 'Empire Blue'
2. *Euonymus europaeus* 'Red Cascade'
3. *Indigofera heterantha*
4. *Buddleja alternifolia*
5. *Olearia* × *haastii* (daisy bush)
6. *Viburnum lantana* (wayfaring tree)
7. *Buxus sempervirens* 'Suffruticosa' x 3 (box)
8. *Santolina chamaecyparissus* x 3 (cotton lavender)
9. *Juniperus scopulorum* 'Skyrocket'
10. *Thalictrum aquilegiifolium* x 5
11. *Campanula glomerata* 'Superba' x 2
12. *Gypsophila paniculata* 'Bristol Fairy' x 3
13. *Linum perenne* x 4 (perennial flax)
14. *Dianthus* 'Alice' x 5
15. *Scabiosa caucasica* 'Clive Greaves' x 5
16. *Dianthus* 'Doris' x 5 (modern pink)
17. *Thalictrum delavayi* 'Hewitt's Double' x 3
18. *Campanula trachelium* x 7 (nettle-leaved bellflower)
19. *Thalictrum aquilegiifolium* var. *album* x 3

Border for Chalky Soil

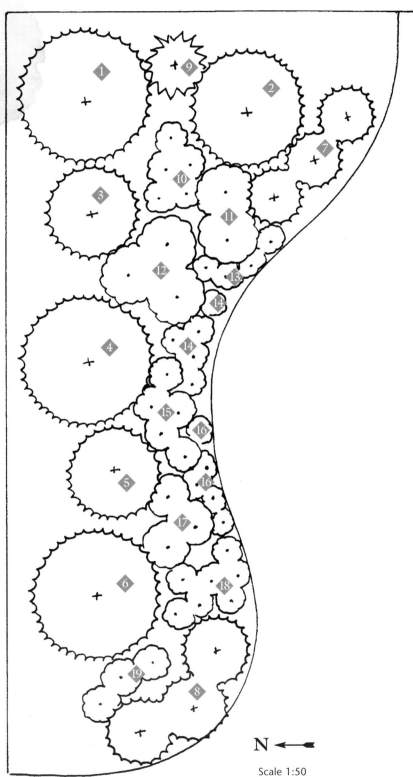

N ←

Scale 1:50

Border for Chalky Soil

Buddleja davidii

Chalky soils tend to drain very easily and are often relatively shallow, a factor which should be borne in mind when selecting plants and preparing the soil. The alkaline nature of these soils does mean that certain plants – such as rhododendrons, camellias and pieris – are difficult to grow satisfactorily. Chemical treatments are available to counteract the yellowing leaves and poor growth of plants which do not thrive in alkaline conditions, but they need to be applied on a long-term basis. It is far better to choose plants which either tolerate a wide range of soil types, or which grow naturally in alkaline soils.

This large south-facing border displays a range of shrubs and herbaceous perennials – together with an impressive conifer – which will indeed grow well in chalky soil; they will also combine interesting combinations of colour and form which complement and contrast with each other. The frothy and feathery flowers are a range of lilacs, blues, pinks and whites, amongst much grey, blue and white-tinged foliage, with touches of yellow and red to brighten the picture.

The border has been designed for a south-facing site, preferably backed by a fence or wall. The ground needs to be prepared really well before planting so, if it has not been cultivated before, it would be worth considering the initial extra effort of breaking up the soil beneath the top spit (spade's depth). It is important to add plenty of organic matter while you dig, to improve the moisture retention of the soil, and advisable to boost the level of organic matter in the soil further by applying a thick mulch after planting. If the soil overlies many

Linum perenne

Euonymus europaeus

metres of solid chalk this is especially necessary as, without these additions the chalk will act like a giant sponge and the soil will dry out too quickly.

Plants and planting

First of all, set out the larger shrubs for the back of the border. Two buddlejas are included in the framework planting. One is a cultivar of the familiar butterfly bush or *Buddleja davidii*. This cultivar, *Buddleja davidii* 'Empire Blue', has large blue-purple flowers with bright orange eyes. These showy clusters of flowers bloom throughout the summer into early autumn. *Buddleja alternifolia* flowers earlier in the summer and has a pleasantly contrasting form, with long arching branches giving a delicate, weeping appearance. Scented lavender-blue flowers are formed in round clusters along the previous year's growth, and attractive, narrow grey-green foliage extends the season of interest. It is often grown as a standard which emphasizes the weeping nature.

Chalky borders are often lacking in plants which give autumn colour but a native plant, the spindle tree or *Euonymus europaeus* is a useful plant for alkaline soils, with its striking red autumn tints. It can be seen growing naturally along chalk downlands with its distinctive four-sided stems and coral-pink berries. *Euonymus europaeus* 'Red Cascade' produces larger red berries with prominent orange seeds.

Indigofera heterantha is a shrubby member of the pea family which can be recognised by its dainty grey-green foliage and purple-pink flowers. The south-facing aspect of this border will suit it well, as would a degree of protection if the border is backed by a wall or fence, which would help it to thrive and flower for a long period throughout the summer.

As a dramatic contrast to these arching shapes, a strong upright conifer has been included. *Juniperus scopulorum* 'Skyrocket' will eventually reach quite a height, but will nevertheless remain very narrow – spreading no more than about 75cm (30in). The form will contrast but the blue-green of the foliage will complement the other soft-coloured flowers.

Olearia × haastii is commonly known as the daisy bush. This rounded, medium-sized shrub is an evergreen with glossy foliage which becomes covered in a mass of fragrant, white, daisy-like flowers in the summer. Another rounded, but deciduous shrub is *Viburnum lantana* or the

Viburnum lantana

Santolina chamaecyparissus

Linum perenne

Campanula trachelium

wayfaring tree. This is a native plant especially suited to chalky soils. Creamy-white flowers appear in clusters in spring to early summer, followed by red berries which turn black. The shoots, buds and undersides of the leaves are covered in a soft down.

Once the larger shrubs are planted, plant the groups of smaller shrubs. Two groups of three, rounded, evergreen shrubs at each end of the border give a sense of rhythm and enclose a mass of herbaceous perennials. *Buxus sempervirens* 'Suffruticosa' is a low-growing box with bright green, glossy foliage and a neat habit. *Santolina chamaecyparissus* has woolly white shoots and silvery foliage, topped by yellow buttons of flowers in the summer.

Herbaceous perennials

When the framework shrubs are in place, you can start planting the infill perennials. Thalictrum and gypsophila give light, frothy, feathery effects in whites and lilacs and have delicate foliage. The bell-shaped flowers of *Campanula glomerata* are a rich purple-blue and are borne in rounded heads, while those of *Campanula trachelium*, or the nettle-leaved bellflower, are more widely spaced on upright stems with serrated foliage. *Linum perenne*, or flax, grows naturally on chalky soils, has bright blue flowers in summer and alternate, narrow leaves on slender stems. The clump-forming *Scabious caucasica* also flowers in the summer, with lilac 'pin-cushion' flowers. Two groups of modern pinks will make low-growing mounds in front of

Buddleja alternifolia, so that the weeping shape of the latter can be appreciated. Flowering over a long period throughout the summer, *Dianthus* 'Alice' has attractive crimson and white flowers, and *D.* 'Doris' is pink with a darker centre.

Aftercare

It is important to give this border an annual mulch, either of compost or well-rotted manure. Apart from the buddlejas, most of the shrubs require minimal pruning, i.e. no regular pruning apart from the routine removal of any dead, damaged or diseased material.

Pruning *Buddleja davidii*

If this shrub is left unpruned, it will produce a mass of lanky stems with poor flowers. Hard pruning every year will make a stronger, balanced shrub, with much larger flowers. The aim is to produce a woody framework about 90cm (36in) high to cut back to each year for new flowering stems. Flowers are produced on the current year's growth.

1 The first spring after planting, cut back the main stem by half to three quarters to produce the framework. Cut out all other growth.

2 The following spring, cut back all growth from the framework to about 5cm (2in) or to one or two pairs of buds. Shorten any branches from the base in line with the framework.

3 In subsequent years, carry on cutting back hard every spring and thin out any overcrowded stems. When the plant is older, encourage new growth for the framework by cutting out one or two older stems right to the ground.

If you have a particularly windy site, shorten the long stems by half in the autumn to prevent wind rock.

Buddleja alternifolia

Unlike *B. davidii*, this shrub flowers on wood produced in the previous growing season. It should therefore be pruned straight after flowering. This will allow the plant to produce strong, new flowering shoots for the following

Dianthus 'Doris'

year. Cut back the stems which have flowered by about one third to strong new growth.

To grow it as a weeping standard use the following method:

1 Select a plant with a strong main stem.

2 Tie the stem to a cane.

3 Pinch back the side shoots to 2–3 leaves, leaving some near the tip. Continue pinching out unwanted side shoots as the stem grows.

4 When it has reached the desired height – about 2m (6ft 6in) – pinch out the end shoot. It will then produce a lot of shoots for a head.

5 For a good, balanced shape, shorten these new shoots in early spring to 15cm (6in). New side growths will grow from these, of which two or three should be selected from each.

6 Once the shape is established, prune normally every year after flowering.

Another shrub which will benefit from regular pruning is *Santolina chamaecyparissus*. Left unpruned these are inclined to become straggly, so a trim after flowering each year will keep the rounded shapes. For an even neater appearance, cut them back hard in spring, to where you can see the new growth beginning to shoot.

Selected plants:

1. *Hamamelis* × *intermedia* 'Diane' (witch hazel)
2. *Pieris* 'Forest Flame'
3. *Hamamelis* × *intermedia* 'Pallida' (witch hazel)
4. *Rhododendron* 'Doncaster'
5. *Skimmia japonica* 'Fragrans' x 2
6. *Gaultheria shallon* x 2 (shallon)
7. *Enkianthus perulatus*
8. *Kalmia latifolia* (calico bush)
9. *Skimmia japonica* 'Nymans' x 2
10. *Rhododendron luteum*

Island Bed for
Acid Soil

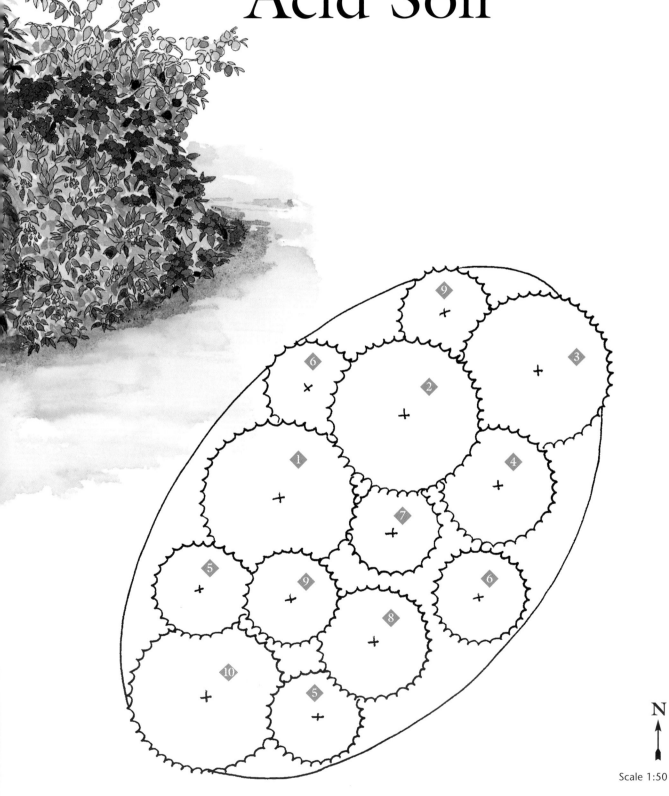

N

Scale 1:50

Island Bed for Acid Soil

Gardening on acid soil gives you the opportunity to grow many different plants, often with rich, colourful displays of flowers and foliage. This large island bed is planted with a mixture of deciduous and evergreen shrubs, all of which are suitable for an acid soil, and most of which specifically require such conditions. It would be possible to create an impressive display by planting with one genus alone, such as rhododendron with its vast array of colours and sizes. However, I have included a range of shrubs for a variety of form and texture.

Site

Choose an area of dappled shade for this bed. The soil should be moisture retentive but well drained. It is important to keep the soil well supplied with organic matter – a regular mulch of leaf mould would be particularly suitable. Do not use any composts or organic matter containing lime, for example mushroom compost, and, if you are buying bags of a compost mix for planting, make sure it is an ericaceous compost as this will be lime-free.

Plants and planting

Set out some of the plants which will grow the largest first of all. The hamamelis, pieris and *Rhododendron luteum* will roughly form a backbone for the bed. When you plant an island bed you need to consider heights, but it is important not to be too rigid in staging plants in tiers, as this tends to give an artificial appearance.

Hamamelis, or witch hazels, are deciduous, spreading shrubs which are particularly valuable for their unusual spidery flowers, borne on bare branches from winter to early spring. *Hamamelis*

Hamamelis × intermedia 'Diane'

× intermedia 'Diane' has deep red flowers, those of *H. × intermedia* 'Pallida' are a golden yellow. Likewise in autumn, the leaves of *H. × intermedia* 'Diane' turn a strong red, and those of *H. × intermedia* 'Pallida' turn a rich yellow.

Pieris 'Forest Flame' is a spectacular evergreen with all year interest, providing a more upright form against the witch hazels. The new foliage in spring is a bright red which changes first to pink, through to cream and then green as the seasons progress. Also in spring, drooping panicles of white flowers contrast with the new red shoots.

Rhododendron luteum is more commonly known as an azalea. It is deciduous with an open habit, thus giving a lighter, airy form compared with the evergreens. From mid- to late spring large clusters of yellow, funnel-shaped flowers, with a mellowing orange touch, cover the shrub and emit a glorious scent. The shrub is again spectacular in the autumn with vivid red foliage.

Next set out the remaining shrubs:
Rhododendron 'Doncaster' is a compact evergreen shrub with glossy, leathery dark green leaves which, in late spring to early summer, is covered in trusses of dark red flowers.

Rhododendron luteum

Skimmia japonica

Enkianthus perulatus provides a lighter, more erect form. A deciduous shrub, it has small elliptical leaves which turn a vivid scarlet in the autumn and creamy-white, urn-shaped flowers are borne in the spring.

   Kalmia latifolia, or the calico bush, has a very similar appearance to a rhododendron. In early summer it is covered with exquisitely marked and shaped, candy pink flowers set against glossy foliage.

   Gaultheria shallon is a spreading, evergreen shrub with dark, pointed leaves and a somewhat jointed appearance. It has urn-shaped, pink flowers in late spring to early summer followed by dark purple berries in autumn to winter.

   Skimmias form very neat, rounded shapes with glossy, aromatic, evergreen foliage. For most of the skimmias, to produce the attractive berries, male plants are needed to pollinate the

females. A ratio of one male to three females will generally be sufficient. However, some of the males are very attractive and worth growing in their own right. *Skimmia japonica* 'Fragrans' is a very free-flowering male form, producing masses of white flowers in the spring which have a strong lily of the valley-like smell. *Skimmia japonica* 'Nymans' is a female form which produces a profusion of relatively large, shiny, red berries.

Other plants suitable for an acid soil

Shrubs
Camellia
Vaccinium
Gaultheria mucronata (syn. *Pernettya mucronata*)
Leucothoe
Corylopsis
Andromeda polifolia
Calluna
Erica cinerea
Daboecia
Cornus canadensis

Herbaceous perennials
Meconopsis betonicifolia
Corydalis cashmeriana
Lithodora diffusa

Flowers of *Enkianthus perulatus*

Selected plants:

1. *Philadelphus* 'Belle Etoile'
2. *Cornus alba* 'Spaethii' x 3
3. *Potentilla fruticosa* 'Tilford Cream' x 2
4. *Mahonia × media* 'Charity'
5. *Potentilla fruticosa* 'Elizabeth'
6. *Hypericum* 'Hidcote'
7. *Primula* Polyanthus x 14
8. *Astilbe × arendsii* 'Fanal' x 2
9. *Lysimachia punctata* x 5
   (garden loosestrife)

Border
for Clay Soil

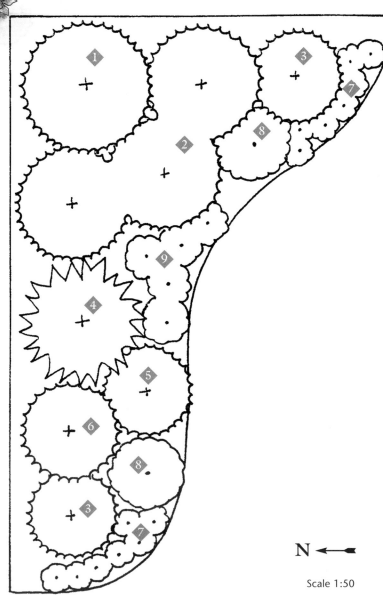

N ←

Scale 1:50

Border for Clay Soil

Clay soils tend to be heavy, cold and badly aerated, so can cause problems for gardeners. However, clay has the advantage of being rich in plant nutrients and much can be done to improve the soil structure:

- Incorporate large quantities of organic matter, choosing drier manures such as well-rotted horse manure or mushroom compost

- Add grit or coarse sand to improve the drainage

- Test the pH of the soil and add lime if necessary

- Never tread on the soil or work on it if it is very wet or dry

Preparation of border

It is important to prepare the border well in advance of planting. First, mark out the border and clear any perennial weeds. Turf or other vegetation which is not seeding may be buried in the bottom of the trench while digging, but make sure the turf is chopped up well. If possible, dig over in the autumn, incorporating plenty of organic matter as you go. Grit or coarse sand can also be mixed in at this stage. Dig with a spade and leave large clods of earth exposed to the air. The frosts over winter will help to break up the soil, doing some of the heavy work for you.

In early spring fork over the border to break up the clods further, using the back of the fork to break up any particularly hard lumps. Don't turn the soil over again, but aim to produce smaller crumbs of soil and a roughly level surface.

Plants and planting

Many plants tolerate a wide range of soil conditions and others thrive particularly well in clay soils. In this border, I have included a mixture of shrubs and perennials suitable for clay soils in a simple, but effective, planting scheme which will provide seasonal interest and contrasting forms.

Take extra care when planting in a clay soil, to make sure that air pockets are not left around the root ball. To help prevent this, a planting mix of

Mahonia × *media* '**Charity**'

74

Primula **Polyanthus**

The perennials can be planted next: a touch of deep red is brought into the scheme with the feathery plumes of *Astilbe* × *arendsii* 'Fanal'. Upright spikes of yellow flowers are provided by *Lysimachia punctata*, while polyanthus are available in a wide range of colours and will give the border a bright lift in the spring. Although they are strictly perennials, they are often better grown as biennials.

Pruning

This border is fairly low maintenance, but some of the shrubs will benefit from regular pruning:

Philadelphus
After it has finished flowering, cut back those stems which have flowered. As the shrub gets older, cut back a few of the older, woody stems right to the base each year but take care to retain the young shoots which will bear the next summer's flowers.

Cornus
To prevent a mass of untidy growth, and to promote the brightest of winter stems, cut hard back each spring to within 5–8cm (2–3in) of the ground. Mulch well after this hard pruning.

Hypericum
Prune in early spring, cutting back to within a few buds of the previous year's growth. When the plant is well established, this is more easily achieved with shears, following the rounded contours of the bush.

compost is particularly useful – place it in the bottom of the planting hole and gently fill in around the plant.

Plant the larger shrubs first: *Philadelphus* 'Belle Etoile' is a tall-growing, deciduous shrub with arching stems and in early to mid-summer these are covered with scented, white, single flowers which are pink at the base.

Mahonia × *media* 'Charity' is an evergreen, giving structure to the border with spiky, glossy foliage and upright racemes of yellow flowers in the winter.

A group of three *Cornus alba* 'Spaethii' provide a mass of golden variegated summer foliage and bright red winter stems.

Hypericum 'Hidcote' is a semi-evergreen, rounded shrub which is covered with bright yellow, saucer-shaped flowers in the summer. These often last well into the autumn.

Potentilla fruticosa 'Elizabeth' and *P. fruticosa* 'Tilford Cream' give a long-lasting display of flowers from late spring to autumn, in yellow and cream respectively, followed by an attractive, brown, twiggy framework over winter.

Other plants suitable for a clay soil

Cotoneaster
Chaenomeles (flowering quince)
Pyracantha (firethorn)
Skimmia
Aucuba
Forsythia
Choisya
Berberis (barberry)
Vinca (periwinkle)
Syringa (lilac)
Spiraea
Corylus (hazel)

Lysimachia punctata

Selected plants:

1. Ballerina apple trees x 4
2. Courgette F1 'Gold Rush' x 2
3. Tomato 'Roma' x 3
4. Globe artichokes x 3 (*Cynara scolymus*)
5. Onions and carrots
6. Runner bean 'Painted Lady'

7. Asparagus pea
8. Lettuce 'Lollo Rossa'
9. Swiss chard
10. Lettuce 'Salad Bowl'
11. Beetroot 'Bull's Blood'
12. *Calendula officinalis*
13. *Convolvulus tricolor*
14. *Limnanthes douglasii*

Edible Garden

N

Scale 1:50

Edible Garden

When space is limited and there is neither the time nor luxury of a large, traditional vegetable garden, smaller areas can be designed to be both attractive and productive. Obviously, the choice of vegetable varies with the individual, and the same crop should not be grown in the same place year after year. This is a guide or suggestion, and many variations may take place within the basic framework. The aim is for the garden to not only look good, but also to supply you with a range of wonderful, freshly picked vegetables.

Four restricted forms of apple tree are included to mark the entrances to the garden and various vegetable crops with interesting foliage, form or flowers are combined with the brightly coloured flowering annuals. Not only will the latter enhance the aesthetic value of the garden, but they will also attract beneficial insects into the garden. Hoverflies, for example, will keep pests such as aphids under control.

A circular stepping-stone path, dissected by another curving line of stepping stones, allows for easy access to all the vegetable crops. Dividing the plot into small, productive areas in this way makes it easier to look after, and you do not need to keep walking over the soil, so the structure is protected. Looking after this garden will not be a heavy, time-consuming chore with large patches to dig.

If you wish to spend a bit more time and money at the outset, a more permanent path could be created to the same shape using small pavers but this would need to be properly constructed, with a hardcore base and mortar to set the pavers in.

Preparation

Dig over the site – which measures 6 x 6m (20 x 20ft) – clear any existing vegetation, then level the plot to lay the stepping-stone path. Mark out a circle as for the Herb Garden (see page 87), but to a radius of 1.75m (5ft 9in). Set out the stones for the circle, level them on a layer of sand, then lay out the stones for the dissecting path. Incorporate an 8cm (3in) layer of well-rotted manure or compost into the remaining sections, but bear in mind which crops are to be grown where, as some do not thrive on freshly manured ground.

Plants and planting

Ballerina apple trees
These trees are very suitable for restricted spaces, provide ornamental features and require less pruning than bushy trees, as they grow as a single column with few side branches.

Plant the four trees in suitable conditions in the dormant season, from late autumn to early spring. They will require permanent stakes about 2m (6ft 6in) high.

1 Dig a straight-sided hole large enough to take the tree roots when well spread out, and to the same depth as the soil level was at the nursery or in the container.

2 Break up the soil underneath with a fork.

3 Drive in a stake just off-centre, to a depth of 45cm (18in).

4 Position the tree so that it is close to the stake, without rubbing.

5 Gradually replace the loose soil, adding a handful of bonemeal and firming as you go, to ensure no air pockets are left.

6 Use two rubber buckle-and-spacer ties to secure the tree firmly to the stake – one near the top and the other half way down.

7 Mulch with a 5–8cm (2–3in) layer of compost, in a 1m (3ft) circle around the tree, taking care to keep the mulch clear of the trunk.

Pruning

Tie the main stem of the tree (or leader) in to the stake as it grows, to keep it straight. Prune it back by a third of the new growth every winter until it reaches the top of the stake, then cut back to about 1cm (½in) from its point of origin. Prune the side branches (or laterals) in mid-to-late summer by counting out four to five leaves from the main stem and pruning just beyond this. Any side shoots growing from these laterals should be pruned harder, to about two leaves.

Vegetable crops

Although you may wish to vary this plan according to your particular tastes, the following is a guide to those shown:

Globe Artichoke

This perennial crop requires a well-manured spot with some shelter from strong winds. They are bold architectural plants with their tall stems and spiky foliage and, for this reason, are sometimes grown in a herbaceous or mixed border, both for their form and for the large, purple, thistle flowers. Grown as a vegetable crop, these flowers are picked before they open.

Plant in the spring and mulch, feed and water well until established. Cut the immature flowerheads when they are fleshy, but before the flowers open. They may need some protection over winter, depending on locality, and it is a good idea to cover with the old flowering stems which are cut back in the autumn or, alternatively, cover with a layer of straw. Being a perennial crop, they are left in the same spot, but will need replacing after three years. New plants can be obtained by removing rooted suckers from the base of existing plants in early to mid-spring.

Courgette F1 'Gold Rush'

The bright yellow flowers of courgette plants are a feature in themselves. This cultivar also has attractive bright yellow, smooth fruits. They require a well drained but rich soil and a sunny site.

Either purchase plants for planting out after the last frosts, i.e. around early summer, or raise from seed. Bell cloches are particularly useful to protect the young plants and are now available in plastic as well as the traditional glass.

Sowing indoors

1 Sow mid- to late spring.

2 Fill a 7.5cm (3in) pot with seed compost and gently firm with fingertips.

3 Place two seeds per pot, 2cm (¾in) deep, on their sides.

4 Water in and place in gentle heat.

5 Thin to stronger plant.

6 Harden off before planting out, i.e. gradually acclimatize to colder temperatures.

Seed may also be sown outside, in situ, from late spring. These will benefit from initial protection.

Mulch the plants and keep well watered. Pick the courgettes regularly, while they are still small, i.e. 10–15cm (4–6in). This will keep the plant cropping well, and provide tender and tasty courgettes.

Tomato 'Roma'

The tomato is another frost-tender plant. Either purchase plants for planting in early summer, or raise from seed under gentle heat. Do not sow deep, as these are much smaller seeds – just place on surface of compost and cover with a fine layer of sieved compost. Again, harden off carefully before planting out.

This is a bush tomato, with plum-shaped fruits, and does not require extensive staking, training and tying in. However, the fruits do need to be protected from the soil, and a layer of straw should be placed under the ripening fruits.

Attractive foliage of lettuce and neat rows of onions

Onions and carrots

Choose a spot for these two crops that has not been freshly manured. Growing alternate rows of carrots and onions is a traditional method of helping to prevent carrot fly. It is also important to rotate these crops from year to year.

1 Prepare a seedbed.

2 Make seed drills 13–20mm (½–¾in) deep at a distance of 15cm (6in) apart.

3 Plant onion sets at 15cm (6in) apart.

4 Sow carrot seed thinly.

5 Cover with soil.

Sowing the carrot seed thinly will avoid the need for thinning, and carrots may be pulled as required as they mature. Let the onions dry off properly before lifting.

Runner bean 'Painted Lady'

This is a very attractive, old-fashioned cultivar of runner bean which has bicoloured orange and white flowers. They need some shelter from the wind, and ground which has been well manured. They also need support, and a willow wigwam is one construction which provides both a functional and pleasing feature or, more simply still, you could make wigwam of bamboo canes.

Runner beans are frost tender. Seed may be sown in pots indoors in late spring under gentle heat, then hardened off and planted out in early summer. If you are sowing outdoors, wait until late spring/early summer. As they are large seeds, sow at a depth of 5cm (2in). Erect the wigwam and sow or plant to aim at two plants per cane, or roughly 15cm (6in) apart.

Asparagus pea

This is another crop with attractive flowers, in this case of a rich velvet red, which develop into unusual winged pods. Pick these when young for tender pods, and pick regularly to encourage cropping. Provide support with twiggy sticks and sow outdoors in late spring at a depth of 2.5cm (1in) and 10cm (4in) apart.

Asparagus pea

Asparagus pea

Central area

Colourful patterns are created by edging with two different lettuce cultivars. The frilly leaves of the red lettuce 'Lollo Rossa' contrast with the silver stems and green foliage of Swiss chard, and the green, lobed leaves of the 'Salad Bowl' lettuce contrast with the red of the beetroot.

Lettuces

These two cultivars are 'cut and come again' lettuces – very useful as leaves can be picked as and when required. Sow in drills in a prepared seedbed at a depth of 15mm (⅝in) from mid- to late spring. To achieve an edging, make a curved drill following the line of the path.

'Lollo Rossa' lettuce

'Salad Bowl' lettuce

Swiss chard

Calendula officinalis

Swiss chard and Beetroot 'Bull's Blood'

Sow both in mid-spring, in a prepared seedbed, at a depth of 2cm (¾in). Place groups of three or four seeds at intervals – chard at 35cm (14in), beetroot at 15cm (6in). Thin seedlings to one per station. The stems of the Swiss chard chosen here are silvery, but other bright colours are available for different colour combinations, for example the red stems of 'Ruby Chard' or bright orange and yellow of 'Rainbow Chard'. This beetroot has dark red foliage.

Convolvulus tricolor

Flowers

Calendula officinalis

This hardy plant is easily raised from seed. Sow outdoors either in early autumn or early to mid-spring. The bright orange flowers will liven up the garden and attract bees and hoverflies. They are also sometimes picked as a salad ingredient. Once established they will self-seed readily.

Convolvulus tricolor

This is another hardy annual, but with trumpet-shaped flowers of a rich blue, with white and yellow throats. Sow outdoors in mid-spring, or start off earlier indoors.

Limnanthes douglasii

This is aptly named the poached egg plant, as a profusion of white and yellow flowers cover the light green foliage and it will seed readily throughout the garden.

In general, it is important to keep this garden well weeded, and watered in dry conditions. Application of mulches are particularly beneficial to prevent loss of moisture. Allow the flowers to seed, but keep an eye on them and move plants to suitable positions so that young vegetable seedlings are not crowded out.

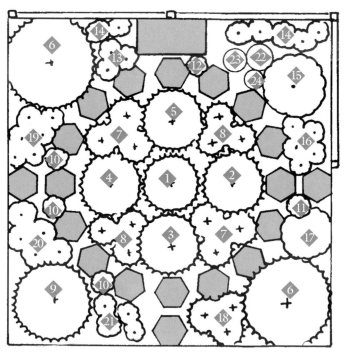

N

Scale 1:50

Herb Garden

Selected plants:

1. *Laurus nobilis* (bay laurel/sweet bay)
2. *Salvia officinalis* (sage)
3. *Salvia officinalis* 'Purpurascens' (sage)
4. *Salvia officinalis* 'Tricolor' (sage)
5. *Salvia officinalis* 'Icterina' (sage)
6. *Rosmarinus officinalis* x 2 (rosemary)
7. *Lavandula angustifolia* 'Hidcote' x 6 (lavender)
8. *Hyssopus officinalis* x 6 (hyssop)
9. *Rosa* The Herbalist™ (rose)
10. *Thymus vulgaris* x 3 (thyme)
11. *Thymus serpyllum* 'Annie Hall' (thyme)
12. *Thymus × citriodorus* 'Silver Queen' (thyme)
13. *Borago officinalis* x 3 (borage)
14. *Helianthus annuus* x 7 (sunflower)
15. *Angelica archangelica* (angelica)
16. *Calendula officinalis* x 5 (pot marigold)
17. *Foeniculum vulgare* 'Purpureum' (bronze fennel)
18. *Origanum vulgare* x 3 (wild marjoram)
19. *Petroselinum crispum* x 6 (parsley)
20. *Allium schoenoprasum* x 5 (chives)
21. *Allium sativum* x 4 (garlic)
22. *Mentha spicata* (common mint)
23. *Mentha suaveolens* (apple mint)
24. *Mentha suaveolens* 'Variegata' (variegated apple mint)

Herb Garden

A herb garden provides an attractive and useful feature in a garden. This design includes a stepping-stone path to wander along as you pick the different herbs, and a seat where you can enjoy this haven of scents, soft foliage and flowers.

A feeling of formality is introduced by a framework of symmetrical planting within a circle of hexagonal stepping stones. This is softened by more relaxed plantings of herbs such as thymes, pot marigolds, parsley and borage, which spread over the stones as they grow.

A clipped bay tree is the centrepiece, providing a strong focal point but an alternative centrepiece could be a stone sun dial or bird bath. This is surrounded by different types of sage, hyssop and lavender. The upright form of the rosemary (*Rosmarinus officinalis*) provides structure in diagonal corners.

Site

Most herbs prefer a sunny site and a well-drained soil. A south-facing aspect would therefore be suitable. To improve drainage, add grit while you are digging the soil, and an extra handful in the planting mix for each plant. Avoid using heavy, rich manures and fertilizers, as most herbs grow naturally in soils which are not very fertile. Neutral to slightly alkaline soil is preferable.

Paving

After thorough preparation the first stage is to lay the hexagonal stones. The ground needs to be firm and level. The plan is based on a 2.5m (8ft) diameter circle in the centre of a plot measuring 4.25 x 4.25m (14 x 14ft).

Mark out the circle in the following way:

1   Knock a post into the centre of the plot, then attach a length of string to it, with a cane on the other end

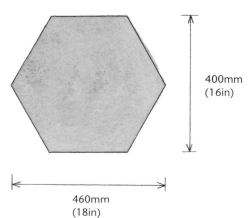

Paving dimension

400mm
(16in)

460mm
(18in)

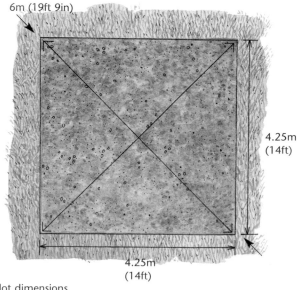

6m (19ft 9in)

4.25m
(14ft)

4.25m
(14ft)

Plot dimensions

Marking out the circle

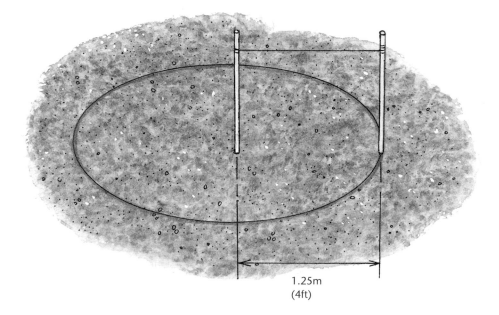

1.25m
(4ft)

2 Adjust the string to achieve a radius of
   1.25m (4ft)

3 Draw the circle by marking the soil with the
   cane, to define the inner area for planting

You can now set out the paving, spacing the
stones evenly around the outside of the circle
and using a spirit level as you work round. A
layer of sand underneath each stone will make
it easier to level. Square slabs may be used as a
base for the seat.

   If the chosen area is not already bounded by
a fence, you can provide seclusion with trellis
along the northern edge of the plot and partly
down one side. Arched trellis panels provide an
attractive feature.

Plants and planting

Framework plants should be planted first, starting
with the central bay laurel tree (*Laurus nobilis*).
In colder districts, either protect the tree during
the winter or plant it in an attractive container and
bring it under cover in the coldest months. You
can buy bay laurels that are already trained and
clipped into a variety of shapes. A ball shape would
complement the circular theme and provide an
instant effect. Alternatively, if you are prepared

to wait longer and are feeling more adventurous
you could train a young tree yourself.

Four different sages surround the bay tree: *Salvia
officinalis*, the common sage, and three cultivars,
which create interesting colour combinations: *S.
officinalis* 'Purpurascens', which is a soft, deep
purple; *S. officinalis* 'Icterina', a bright yellow and
green; *S. officinalis* 'Tricolor', which is variegated
cream, purple and green.

Salvia officinalis 'Tricolor'

Lavandula augustifolia 'Hidcote'

Lavandula angustifolia 'Hidcote' has been chosen here, because it stays more compact than most lavenders and will provide pleasing rounded shapes amongst the more sprawling sages.

Hyssopus officinalis is a semi-evergreen with darker green foliage and spikes of dark blue-purple flowers.

Rosmarinus officinalis, a rosemary with upright green foliage, is another framework plant. The common rosemary does tend to be the hardiest but in colder, more exposed positions,

you may need to protect the plants over the winter. Alternatively, you could plant two roses, which have a long tradition in herb gardens. I have, in any case, included the modern cultivar, *Rosa* The Herbalist™, which looks almost identical to the old-fashioned 'The Apothecarie's Rose' with light crimson, semi-double flowers and golden stamens, yet has the modern attributes of repeat flowering.

Lower growing, framework plants include wild marjoram (*Origanum vulgare*) and a selection of

Rosmarinus officinalis

Angelica archangelica

Allium sativum (chives)

thymes, *Thymus vulgaris, T. serpyllum* 'Annie Hall' and *T.* × *citriodorus* 'Silver Queen', to spread between the paving. These may need replacing every three or four years as they have a tendency to become leggy. Regular, very light pruning throughout the growing season will help to prevent this.

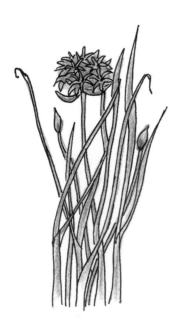

Chives

Two herbs which add interest during the growing season are angelica (*Angelica archangelica*), a short-lived perennial with a strong architectural form, which will readily propagate itself by seeding, and bronze fennel (*Foeniculum vulgare* 'Purpureum'), which provides a very attractive, upright feature with graceful, feathery foliage.

Plants requiring richer soil

Compost or very well-rotted manure should be added to the soil for herbs such as parsley (*Petroselinum crispum*) and chives (*Allium schoenoprasum*).

Chives need to be regularly cut near to the base for a supply of fresh leaves. Strictly speaking, they should not be allowed to flower if grown for culinary purposes. However, the flowers are so attractive that it is worth growing more plants than you need and allowing some to develop flowers. Once established they will benefit from being divided every three or four years.
Parsley is biennial, flowering in its second year.

Borago officinalis (borage)

It will therefore need to be sown or planted every year.

The common mint (*Mentha spicata*) also requires a slightly richer soil, but not too rich because it is so invasive. To keep it in check, plant it in pots and sink them into the ground. Apple mint (*Mentha suaveolens*) has soft, rounded leaves, and with the variegated apple mint (*Mentha suaveolens* 'Variegata') provides a contrast of foliage against the common mint.

Garlic (*Allium sativum*) should be planted in late autumn, if possible in a spot which has had manure or compost applied the year before. Choose good-sized, healthy looking cloves and plant them fairly deep, about 10cm (4in). Make sure the cloves are the right way up, that is with the flat base-plate underneath. For culinary use, lift them for drying when the leaves start to turn yellow.

Annuals

Several annuals, which are easily raised from seed, have been chosen to grow between the framework plants. Pot marigolds (*Calendula officinalis*) brighten up the planting with their cheerful orange flowers and a pleasing contrast will be provided with the blues and greens of the other herbs. They will self seed readily in the herb garden, as will borage (*Borago officinalis*) with its bright blue, star-shaped flowers. Although not traditionally included in herb gardens, sunflowers (*Helianthus annuus*) have been used here to give a bright and cheerful backdrop for the seating area.

Alternative plants

While keeping the basic framework, this plan may be adapted for individual preferences. It is important to grow the herbs that you enjoy using for cooking, so you may wish to use any of the following as infill plants:

Anethum graveolens (dill)
Anthriscus cerefolium (chervil)
Armoracia rusticana (horseradish)
Artemesia dracunculus (French tarragon)
Satureja montana (winter savory)
Levisticum officinale (lovage)
Carum carvi (caraway)
Coriandrum sativum (coriander)

If you have included a trellis, planting climbers such as honeysuckle (lonicera) and the golden hop (*Humulus lupulus* 'Aureus') will bring extra colour and scent to the garden.

Selected plants:

1. *Lavatera plebeia* 'Rosea'
2. *Rosa* Graham Thomas
3. *Buxus sempervirens* 'Suffruticosa Variegata' (variegated box)
4. *Lavandula angustifolia* x 6 (old English lavender)
5. *Rosa* 'Roseraie de l'Haÿ'
6. *Rosmarinus officinalis* (rosemary)
7. *Rosa* Cottage Rose™
8. *Daphne mezereum*
9. *Syringa microphylla* 'Superba'
10. *Campanula persicifolia* 'Telham Beauty' x 3
11. *Digitalis purpurea* x 6 (foxglove)
12. *Achillea ptarmica* 'The Pearl' x 3
13. *Aster* x *frikartii* x 3
14. *Delphinium elatum* x 6
15. *Astrantia major* x 3 (masterwort)
16. *Alchemilla mollis* x 4 (lady's mantle)
17. *Aquilegia vulgaris* 'Nora Barlow' x 3
18. *Geranium* 'Johnson's Blue' x 3
19. *Paeonia lactiflora* 'Bowl of Beauty'
20. *Phlox paniculata* x 6
21. *Lupinus* Russell hybrids x 4
22. *Paeonia lactiflora* 'Félix Crousse'
23. *Dianthus barbatus* (sweet William)
24. *Nigella damascena* (love-in-a-mist)
25. *Centaurea cyanus* (cornflower)
26. *Lathyrus odoratus* (sweet pea)

Cottage
Garden

Scale 1:50

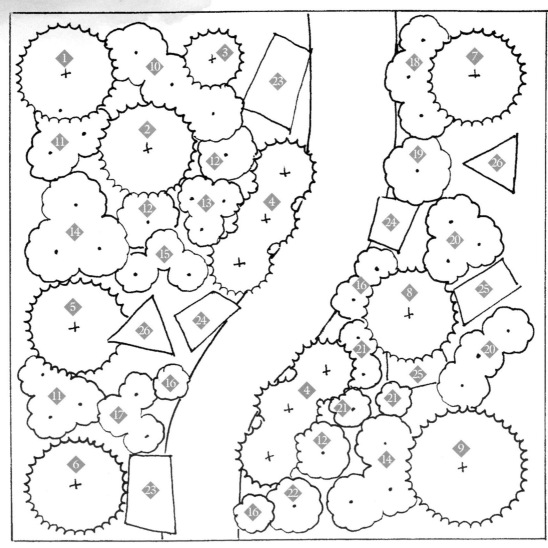

Cottage Garden

The possibilities and combinations of planting in a cottage garden style are endless and here a mixture of shrubs, herbaceous perennials, biennials and annuals are planted with a degree of informality. Allow the plants to spread and seed themselves so that the borders become packed with colour, scent, and hopefully, bees, butterflies and beneficial insects.

Site

This plan is for a fairly sunny position – possibly for a front garden with the path leading from a front gate to front door. The boundaries may be a hedge, fence or wall. If the latter two, planting possibilities are opened up even further by covering them with climbers. Arches may also be introduced over the central path creating further opportunities for vertical planting.

Thorough ground preparation is very important. Clear the site of weeds, taking particular care to remove perennial weeds. This will make it much easier to look after the beds in subsequent years if you allow the chosen plants to spread and self-seed naturally. Dig in a layer of well-rotted manure or compost, preferably in the autumn or winter before planting.

Plants and planting

A few shrubs are included in the plan, while plenty of space has been allowed for a variety of different types of other plants. The idea is that the framework should not be rigid, so there is the opportunity for more choice and experimentation and the garden can grow and develop naturally. If, for example, a new annual or biennial catches your eye, or if you have a particular favourite, there will

Perennials spilling over a garden path

be somewhere to fit it in. If you spot a pleasing colour combination, this can be encouraged the following year. You may also find interesting plants seed themselves from neighbouring gardens or the countryside – they may turn out to be invasive weeds, or you may have interesting plant combinations in your garden for free.

A cottage garden would not be complete without scented roses. *Rosa* Graham Thomas is a fragrant, deep, soft yellow rose with shiny, mid-green foliage, while *Rosa* Cottage Rose™ is a free-flowering, warm-pink rose. Both of these are English roses, which combine an old-fashioned charm with the modern attributes of repeat flowering. *Rosa* 'Roseraie de l'Haÿ' is an exquisitely scented rugosa rose with deep pink-purple, double flowers early in the summer, amidst healthy green foliage. This is a good one to grow as, like most rugosas, it tolerates poorer soils and is not usually affected by black spot. Leave the flowers on and there will be a display of hips in the autumn.

Climbing roses

An evergreen form is provided by planting the variegated box, *Buxus sempervirens* 'Suffruticosa Variegata' and *Rosemarinus officinalis* (rosemary) has an upright, evergreen form with aromatic foliage and blue flowers. *Lavandula angustifolia*, the aromatic English lavender, will spread over

the edge of the path and softens any hard edges with its pale grey-blue flowers and silvery-grey foliage. If three are planted either side of the path, as shown, it will emphasize the curve and lead the eye along the path.

Plant *Daphne mezereum* fairly close to the path in order to appreciate the scent in the winter months. This is a deciduous shrub with upright stems and, in late winter to early spring the bare stems are covered with pink-purple fragrant flowers, followed by red fruits. However, bear in mind that these fruits are poisonous.

Syringa microphylla 'Superba' is a larger, deciduous shrub. Sometimes known as the 'small-leafed lilac', it has delicate, pink flowers in early summer and often again in the autumn.

The mallow, *Lavatera plebeia* 'Rosea', produces an abundance of deep pink flowers throughout the summer. It is a fairly vigorous plant, but may be affected by severe winters. If you cut hard back in the spring it will quickly make new shoots to flower in the summer.

Once the shrubs have been planted, the herbaceous perennials may then be arranged in drifts, or dotted in between. Tall spires of blue will be provided by campanula and delphinium in early to mid-summer. *Campanula persicifolia* 'Telham Beauty' will happily spread throughout the border giving a haze of pale blue and the hybrids of *Delphinium elatum* are available in a wide range of colours, from white and cream to pink, pale blue and purple.

The vertical element is continued with *Lupinus*

Lavatera plebia 'Rosea'

Geranium 'Johnson's Blue'

Russell hybrids. These familiar and cheery summer flowers come in a variety of colours ranging from reds, oranges and yellows, to pinks, blues and white. They are often attractively bi-coloured.

Aquilegia vulgaris 'Nora Barlow' has an old-fashioned feel with double flowers of red, pink and green. This is another useful plant for self-seeding around the garden, but the seedlings are likely to revert to the ordinary 'granny's bonnets' which are nevertheless very attractive.

Achillea ptarmica 'The Pearl' has pompoms of white summer flowers, while _Astrantia major_ has delicate star-like flowers of a greenish-pink and is again summer flowering.

Aster × frikartii flowers later in the summer and into autumn. It has blue daisy flowers with yellow centres. _Phlox paniculata_ also flowers later in the summer with scented deep pink flowers. Named garden cultivars are more likely to be available than the true species, and provide a wider range of colours.

Paeonia lactiflora 'Bowl of Beauty' is a clear pink with a creamy yellow centre, while the blowsy and luxuriant flowers of _Paeonia lactiflora_ 'Félix Crousse' fill the air with a wonderful scent in early summer. This particular cultivar has double flowers of a rich crimson.

Plant the lower-growing perennials to spread over the edges of the path. _Geranium_ 'Johnson's Blue' has attractive divided foliage and bright blue flowers in the summer which complement the pink of the rose. _Alchemilla mollis_ has attractive lobed foliage and frothy, lime green

flowers. The cool, fresh colours combine well with many brighter flowers and it is a useful plant for softening the overall effect and avoiding the clashing of colours. It will also do the work for you, by self-seeding freely.

Biennials

Dianthus barbatus (sweet Williams) are usually grown as biennials, although they will live for longer. Likewise, _Digitalis purpurea_, the foxgloves, are really short-lived perennials which are grown as biennials. Foxgloves are naturally plants for a shadier spot, but seem to grow quite happily in other conditions and will seed themselves from year to year.

Leaf of _Alchemilla mollis_

Nigella damascena

Annuals

The annuals for this plan are all hardy and therefore may be sown directly into the open ground in spring. *Nigella damascena* (love-in-a-mist) gives a haze of soft blue flowers followed by interesting seed-heads. You will only need to sow these in the first year as they will self-seed easily in following years. *Centaurea cyanus* (cornflower) is a taller annual with the familiar cornflower blue flowers held high on wiry stems.

The *Lathyrus odoratus* (sweet peas) will need some form of support – a simple wigwam of bamboo canes may be constructed, or a more elaborate support such as willow may be used. The seeds may be sown directly in the ground in the spring, or indoors in pots for earlier flowers.

Sowing in pots
- To aid germination of the dark coloured seeds nick the seed coat with a sharp knife
- Add extra grit to the seed compost to aid drainage
- Sow two or three seeds to a 7.5cm (3in) pot
- In mild districts sow in autumn
- Leave in greenhouse or indoors to germinate
- Place in cold frame over winter
- In colder areas sow in late winter to early spring
- Plant out from mid- to late spring, positioning plants to one side of supports
- Pick regularly to encourage flowering

Staking
As the approach is informal little staking is necessary, but the large flowerheads of delphiniums, *Delphinium elatum*, are likely to require some support. Put stakes or supports in place in the spring so that the flower spikes can be supported as they grow.

Deadheading
Most of the plants will benefit from deadheading unless – as is the case with the rugosa rose – fruits are expected in the autumn. Nigella may be left for their attractive seedheads, and foxgloves may be left to self-seed. For plants such as the other roses, campanulas and lupins deadheading will encourage them to carry on flowering. For others, it will mean that the energy is put back into the plant rather than in seed production, making stronger, healthier plants.

Lathyrus odoratus

Selected plants:

1. *Ilex aquifolium* (holly)
2. *Corylus avellana* (hazel)
3. *Symphoricarpos albus* (snowberry)
4. *Lavandula angustifolia* x 6 (old English lavender)
5. *Buddleja davidii* (butterfly bush)
6. *Ribes sanguineum* (flowering currant)
7. *Sedum spectabile* x 12 (ice plant)
8. *Aster × frikartii* x 5
9. *Achillea millefolium* x 5 (yarrow)
10. *Thymus serpyllum* x 7 (wild thyme)
11. *Filipendula ulmaria* x 7 (meadowsweet)
12. *Lythrum salicaria* x 5 (purple loosestrife)
13. *Persicaria bistorta* x 5 (bistort)
14. *Eupatorium cannabinum* x 3 (hemp agrimony)
15. *Ajuga reptans* 'Atropurpurea' x 5
16. *Anthriscus sylvestris* (cow parsley)
17. *Convallaria majalis* (lily of the valley)
18. *Echium vulgare* (viper's bugloss)
19. *Dipsacus fullonum* (teasel)

Garden
for Wildlife

Hedge

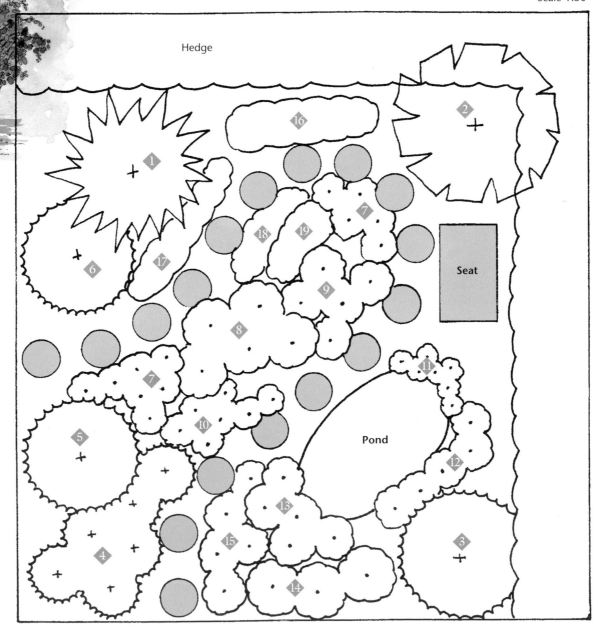

16

2

1

7

18   19

6

17

9

Seat

8

7

11

5

10

Pond

12

4

13

15

3

14

Garden for Wildlife

This garden is informal and relaxed. A stepping-stone path meanders through the plants past a rustic bench, where you can sit and observe the pondlife, birds and insects.

To attract wildlife to your garden you will need to create a wide range of habitats with areas of shelter. In contrast to most traditional gardening methods, care must be taken not to be too tidy, as piles of decaying leaves and twigs will provide habitats for many insects. Avoid plants which have been highly bred, such as double-flowered forms, as these are likely to be lacking in pollen and nectar, or difficult for insects to visit.

The following features have been chosen to attract wildlife to this garden:

- A hedgerow of native species, to provide shelter, food and a nesting site for birds
- A pond to provide a habitat for aquatic life and a water supply for other creatures
- Plants, such as sedum, buddleja and asters to attract butterflies
- Plants, such as teasels and holly, for birds
- Plants, such as lavender and thyme, for bees
- Native species, such as the wild flowers *Lythrum salicaria* (purple loosestrife), *Filipendula ulmaria* (meadowsweet) and *Anthriscus sylvestris* (cow parsley)

The first step towards creating this garden is to plant the hedge:

Hedgerow

A hedge is a long-term project, so it is worth spending time at the outset to prepare the site well. Using a garden line, mark out the position for the hedge. Prepare the ground to a width of at least 1m (3ft) by the length of the hedge. Clear any weeds, taking particular care to remove the roots of any perennial weeds, and dig out a trench to the depth of a spade. If the subsoil is compacted, fork this to break

Asters attracting butterflies

Lythrum salicaria

Several different hedging plants are suitable, but for this garden I suggest:

Crataegus monogyna x 35 (hawthorn)
Prunus spinosa x 15 (blackthorn)
Acer campestre x 10 (field maple)
Viburnum opulus x 5 (guelder rose)
Viburnum lantana x 5 (wayfaring tree)

Set the hedging plants out in double, staggered rows and plant at the same depth as they were in the nursery, firming in well. To encourage bushiness, trim both the leading branches and side branches by about one third after planting and mulch the plants. In subsequent years mulch the hedge every spring.

Trim the hedge as late as possible in the year. No hedge should be clipped while birds may still be nesting from spring to early summer, but this is particularly important for a hedge planted specifically to encourage wildlife.

Viburnum lantana

it up but do not mix the two layers. Place a layer of well-rotted manure or compost in the trench and replace the top soil, mixing together with the compost.

Hedging plants are very often available in the dormant season as bare-rooted 'whips'. They may be planted in suitable conditions between late autumn and early spring, but late autumn is preferable. If the plants have dried out, soak them in a bucket of water for a couple of hours before planting.

Planting a hedge

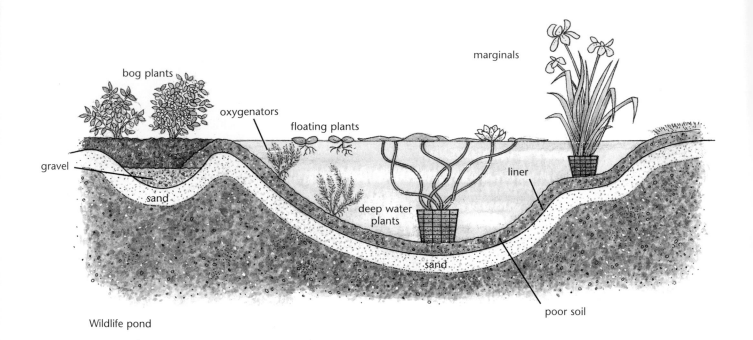

bog plants

oxygenators

marginals

floating plants

gravel

sand

liner

deep water plants

sand

poor soil

Wildlife pond

Trimming should therefore be delayed until late summer/early autumn and through to the winter for plants such as hawthorn which bear berries. Although this is an informal hedge that does not require clipping into rigid shapes, take care to encourage a bushy shape which is wider at the base. This will prevent long straggly growth breaking under the weight of snow.

Pond

A source of water is of great importance in a wildlife garden but, if you do not wish to install a pond, place a low bird bath or trough in this area and increase the number of plants. Although this will not provide the breeding ground for creatures such as frogs and newts, it will provide a valuable source of drinking water.

The pond for this garden is about 2.5 x 1.4m (8 x 4ft 6in) and should be at least 60cm (2ft) deep at the centre. This will allow an ice-free zone in the winter to protect pond life. It should have gently sloping sides to allow access for creatures such as hedgehogs to drink and scavenge on pond snails, without falling in and drowning.

There are two basic options for creating a pond – either a pre-formed liner or a flexible liner. If you decide on a pre-formed liner, select one designed specifically for wildlife, as ledges

will be incorporated for marginal plants, and the sides will be gently sloping. A flexible liner is a less expensive option which may take longer to install, but allows for more scope in design and choice of sizes.

Installing a flexible liner

1 Mark out the shape using a rope or garden hose.
2 Dig out the hole to the required depth, allowing shallow shelves for marginal plants and gently sloping sides.
3 Using a spirit level, check that the top is level, otherwise you will have an expanse of liner showing.
4 Remove any sharp stones or debris.
5 Place a layer of matting or 5cm (2in) of sand as an underlay for the liner.
6 Drape the liner over this, fitting it into the shape.
7 Place a 5–8cm (2–3in) layer of poor or subsoil over the bottom. Do not use rich top soil, or any manure or compost.
8 Gradually fill with water, moulding the liner into position as you go.
9 Create boggy areas at the sides by burying sections of liner.
10 If available, add a bucketful of water from an established (but healthy) pond. This will aid the colonization of wildlife.
11 Leave for at least a week before planting.

Plant selection for pond

A balance of aquatic plants is important for a healthy pond. Choose a selection of native species, including deep water, floating, oxygenating and marginal plants. A suggested mix for this size of pond would be:

- 35 x oxygenating plants, such as *Myriophyllum spicatum* (spiked water milfoil) and *Ceratophyllum demersum* (rigid hornwort)
- 4 x floating plants such as *Stratiotes aloides* (water soldier)
- 12 x marginal plants such as *Mentha aquatica* (water mint), *Caltha palustris* (marsh marigold) and *Menyanthes trifoliata* (bogbean).
- 2 x deep water plants such as *Nymphoides peltata* (fringed water lily)

Planting should take place in the growing season, i.e. from late spring to early autumn. The floating plants are simply dropped into the water. Oxygenating plants may be treated in the same way, but in weighted bunches. Use special planting baskets and poor soil or aquatic compost for the marginal plants and deep water plants. Place the marginal plants on the ledges specially prepared for them and the deep water plants further towards the centre.

Once these two major features have been positioned, the next stage is to set out the informal path.

Caltha palustris

Stepping-stone path

Choose circular or irregular-shaped stepping stones for this garden. Log stepping stones would be in keeping, but as these become very slippery and need to be covered with a wire mesh, log-effect stone is a better option. Set the stones out and walk round to check that they suit your stride. Firm and level the ground underneath and place a little sand underneath to help bed the stones in.

Nymphoides peltata

Hazel catkins

Once the basic structure of the garden is in place the plants can be introduced. Plant the two native trees first – the well-known holly (*Ilex aquifolium*) and hazel (*Corylus avellana*). Then plant the shrubs. Some non-native species of shrubs and perennials have been included as they are attractive to a vast range of butterflies, bees, hoverflies and other insects.

Ribes sanguineum (flowering currant) is an early flowering shrub with deep pink, tubular flowers in early to mid-spring, followed by black fruits. *Symphoricarpos albus* is a twiggy, suckering shrub. The small pink flowers attract a myriad of bees and insects and are followed by marble-like, white fruits giving it the common name of snowberry. Planted to the back of the pond, it provides shelter for creatures, and links up with the hedge to give a protected run between water and hedge.

Buddleja davidii is very aptly named the butterfly bush, as it attracts a myriad of butterflies and bees. It flowers in the summer, when the mass of purple flowers from the group of lavenders (*Lavandula angustifolia*) planted nearby will also be alive with bees and insects.

Once the shrubs have been planted, the next step is to position the perennials. Plant in bold but informal groups and drifts to spread over the central area. *Aster × frikartii* is a single-flowered aster with lavender blue flowers in late summer to autumn. *Sedum spectabile* has flattish heads of deep pink flowers, which are very attractive to butterflies. Leave the attractive, brown seed heads on over winter. *Achillea millefolium* (yarrow) is a

spreading perennial with feathery foliage and flowers in white or a range of colours, attractive to a variety of insect life.

Four perennials which require damp conditions are included around the pond area; plant these in a boggy area created by the edges of the pond liner. *Filipendula ulmaria* (meadowsweet), *Lythrum salicaria* (purple loosestrife), *Persicaria bistorta* (bistort) and

Buddleja davidii

Persicaria bistorta

Eupatorium cannabinum (hemp agrimony) are all native species. Meadowsweet has frothy cream-white flowers. Both purple loosestrife and bistort have spikes of flowers which are purple and pink respectively. Hemp agrimony is topped with dense clusters of purplish pink flowers.

Ajuga reptans 'Atropurpurea' is a low-growing perennial which will carpet the ground. Blue spikes of flowers are borne above the dense, dark purple foliage from late spring to early summer.

Anthriscus sylvestris is the well-known cow parsley, which may be regarded as a troublesome weed. However, the frothy white flowers against the hedgerow hedge in late spring to early summer make for one of the most pleasing combinations.

Convallaria majalis (lily of the valley) will spread rapidly by the holly tree, with fragrant white flowers in spring. *Echium vulgare* (viper's bugloss) has pinkish flowers turning to blue which are much loved by bees. *Dipsacus fullonum* (teasel) is easily raised by seed, and can be allowed to spread itself around the garden by self-seeding. The tall thistle-like seedheads are particularly attractive for goldfinches.

Wild flowers in general should be allowed to seed and spread themselves throughout the garden and a patch of plants such as nettles or comfrey will make a valuable contribution, by attracting butterflies and bees. Obviously, though, a certain amount of control is needed to keep a pleasant and good mix of plants without one species dominating.

Dipsacus fullonum

Selected plants:

1. *Miscanthus sinensis* 'Gracillimus' x 12
2. *Deschampsia cespitosa* 'Goldschleier' x 3
3. *Deschampsia cespitosa* 'Bronzeschleier' x 3
4. *Achillea millefolium* x 6 (yarrow)
5. *Sedum* 'Herbstfreude' x 8
6. *Anaphalis margaritacea* x 6
7. *Alchemilla mollis* x 3 (lady's mantle)
8. *Achillea ptarmica* 'The Pearl' x 2
9. *Anthemis tinctoria* 'E.C. Buxton' x 3

Meadow-effect
Island Bed

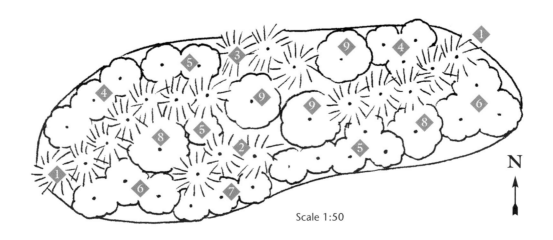

Scale 1:50

N

Meadow-effect Island Bed

If you are looking for a less structured and more natural appearance for your garden, the soft, flowing effect of this meadow-style planting is a good option. Plants are not tiered and grouped strictly according to height, instead long drifts of grasses move across the bed, the slightest breeze bringing them alive. No shrubs or trees are included but, by leaving seedheads on, the bed remains attractive throughout autumn and winter. Plants may be allowed to spread according to their natural means, although a little stage management may be necessary to achieve a pleasing balance. Plants may also be allowed to seed throughout the bed, but avoid introducing too many different types of plants as this would give a cluttered and bitty appearance. The overall effect should be simple and flowing. The main seasons of interest are summer, autumn and winter.

Site and preparation

This island bed would be equally at home in a lawn or surrounded by a gravel area. Clear and dig over the bed in the autumn or winter, incorporating organic material. Do not use over-rich manures as too rich a soil may result in a lot of leafy growth at the expense of the grasses flowering; garden compost or composted bark would be suitable.

Plants and planting

Planting is best carried out in the spring, provided there is no frost and the soil is neither too wet nor too dry.

A vast array of attractive and interesting grasses is available, and the temptation is to include as many different types as possible. While that would

Grasses bring movement to a garden

be useful for a botanical collection, to create a meadow effect, the choice should be restricted.

Plant the grasses first

Miscanthus sinensis 'Gracillimus' is a slender, graceful species, growing to about 1.25m (4ft) in height. Plant two long sweeping drifts of this perennial grass, right to the edges of the bed. Pale, silvery spikelets are produced in the early autumn and last through the winter, while the foliage turns an attractive bronze colour.

Deschampsia cespitosa is an evergreen, tuft-forming grass with clumps of upright foliage. Soft, dainty flowerheads form in the summer and also last through the winter. Two groups of

Seed heads of *Sedum* 'Herbstfreude'

different cultivars are included – *D. cespitosa* 'Bronzeschleier' and *D. cespitosa* 'Goldschleier', with bronze and gold foliage effects respectively.

Next, position the herbaceous perennials to both complement and contrast with the bold drifts and clumps of the grasses.

Achillea millefolium is a spreading plant which provides a horizontal line of flat flowerheads, to contrast with the upright form of the grasses. Many different-coloured cultivars are available, including striking reds and subtle shades of bronze, orange, yellow and cream. The contrast in form is also achieved with the flat, pink flowerheads of *Sedum* 'Herbstfreude', which turn an attractive russet brown over winter.

Anaphalis margaritacea has silvery grey foliage and heads of small white flowers in the summer. Leave the flowerheads on for a silvery effect over winter.

Alchemilla mollis has fresh green, attractively lobed foliage and frothy yellow/green flowers in the summer. The colouring echoes that of the golden foliage of the golden deschampsia, but the rounded form contrasts. Allow this plant to seed throughout the bed.

Achillea ptarmica 'The Pearl' has wiry stems and narrow, dark green foliage topped with pompoms of white flowers in the summer. Allow a certain amount of natural spread, but this plant may become invasive and care must be taken that it does not take over nearby plants.

Anthemis tinctoria 'E.C. Buxton' brings a mass of pale yellow, daisy-like flowers to the bed in the summer.

Do not be in a hurry to tidy up this border – leave any cutting back to the spring, otherwise you will miss a wonderful winter display; the seedheads are shown off particularly well on frosty, bright days.

In the spring, cut back the herbaceous plants close to ground level, or to healthy, new growth. Apply a layer of mulch to the bed, such as bark chippings or well-rotted compost.

Other suitable plants

Festuca glauca
Miscanthus sinensis 'Zebrinus'
Aster turbinellus
Rudbeckia 'Goldsturm'
Echinacea purpurea
Miscanthus sinensis 'Silberfeder'

Anthemis tinctoria 'E.C. Buxton'

Selected plants:

1. *Darmera peltata* (umbrella plant)
2. *Filipendula rubra*
3. *Rodgersia aesculifolia* x 6
4. *Iris laevigata* 'Alba' x 2
5. *Iris laevigata* x 5
6. *Lysichiton americanus* x 3 (yellow skunk cabbage)

Bog Garden

Scale 1:50

N

Bog Garden

Permanently boggy areas in the garden present a problem for most plants, but there are many plants which actually require such conditions. So, rather than going to the expense and effort of draining the land, why not take advantage of the situation and grow a different range of plants? On the other hand, if your garden has no damp areas and you wish to grow bog garden plants, you can create a boggy area. A particularly appropriate site would be next to an existing pond. This is easily achieved with the use of a pond liner:

1 Dig a hole to a depth of at least 45cm (18in) with sloping sides, to the appropriate dimensions.

2 Lay a flexible liner in the hole and tuck the sides of the liner into the surrounding soil so it is just below ground level.

3 Pierce small holes in the liner, a 1cm (½in) hole every 1m (3ft) is sufficient, to prevent stagnant conditions.

4 Place a layer of gravel over the holes to prevent them from becoming blocked.

5 Fill with soil.

This plan is for quite a large bog garden, with a maximum length and width of about 5.5 x 3m (18 x 10ft); but the same principles apply if you wish to create a smaller bog garden. Alternative species are suggested for some plants for a smaller area. Single plants, or smaller groups of the other plants may be used.

Rodgersia aesculifolia

Plants and planting

Plants for a bog garden include some unusual plants, ranging from the delicate and pretty to the weird and wonderful. This is not a garden for the winter months as, although the plants are perennials, most of them die back over the winter. There is, however, a span of changing interest from spring to autumn.

Plant in the spring, making sure the area is well soaked before planting and keep the bog garden well watered in dry conditions throughout the growing season.

Darmera peltata (syn. *Peltiphyllum peltatum*) is a spreading plant with a strange flowering habit. Long flower stalks appear in the spring before the foliage, with heads of pink-white flowers. Rounded, umbrella-like leaves follow, which have reddish-brown autumn colours. If adapting this plan for a smaller area, choose the more compact cultivar, *Darmera peltata* 'Nana'.

Many bog plants are quite dramatic, and

Vertical form of iris

Filipendula rubra provides rapid height for the garden, with upright stems up to 2–2.5m (6ft 6in–8ft) topped with feathery, pink flowers in the summer.

Interesting foliage is a feature of *Rodgersia aesculifolia*. The horse chestnut-like leaves are an attractive green with bronze tinges, and the plumes of summer flowers are pinkish-white.

A band of spiky foliage running across the centre of the bog garden is achieved by planting *Iris laevigata*. This spreading plant has tall stems of blue flowers striped with yellow, while *I. laevigata* 'Alba' is the white-flowered cultivar. Both are summer flowering.

Perhaps the most unusual plant in the bog garden is *Lysichiton americanus* or the skunk cabbage – definitely not a plant to grow near the house for a pleasant scent! In the spring, striking spathes of bright yellow are produced, before the long green leaves appear. This is

another spreading plant, seeding readily. If a less invasive species is required for a smaller area, choose *Lysichiton camtschatcensis* which has smaller, white spathes.

Aftercare

The bog garden must not be allowed to dry out so, if dry conditions occur during the growing season, water well, soaking the area. A mulch of organic matter applied in the spring will benefit the plants and help conserve moisture. Some of the more vigorous, invasive plants may need to be kept in check to make sure that others are not swamped.

Other bog garden plants

Filipendula ulmaria (meadowsweet)
Gunnera manicata
Eupatorium cannabinum (hemp agrimony)
Astilbe × arendsii
Lythrum salicaria (purple loosestrife)
Ligularia przewalskii

Lysichiton americanus

Selected plants:

1. *Sarcococca hookeriana* var. *digyna* x 2
2. *Ruscus aculeatus* x 4 (butcher's broom)
3. *Doronicum pardalianches*
   (leopard's bane)
4. *Anemone hupehensis* x 3
5. *Anemone × hybrida* 'Honorine Jobert'
6. *Dicentra spectabilis* (bleeding heart)
7. *Pulmonaria saccharata* x 10

Planted in drifts :

8. *Anemone nemorosa* 'Robinsoniana'
9. *Primula vulgaris* (primrose)
10. *Viola riviniana* (common dog violet)

Woodland Edge – Shady Border

N

Scale 1:50

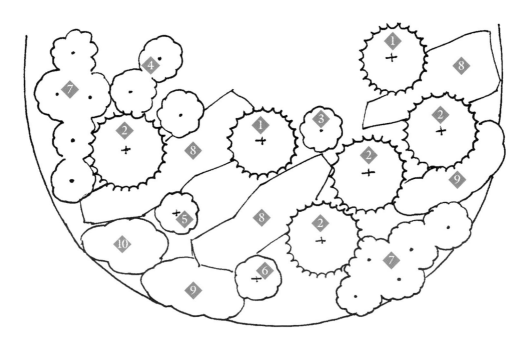

Woodland Edge – Shady Border

A shady area in the garden need not be a problem area, as it opens up many possibilities for different plans and provides the opportunity to grow plants which have adapted to live under the shade of trees. These include many of our native spring flowers – such as wood anemones, wood sorrel and primroses – which take advantage of the dappled light available in a deciduous woodland by flowering before the leaves unfurl and cast a heavier shade.

The border is less structured than many, to give the feel of a natural woodland edge. Plants need not be strictly tiered by height, but placed more randomly and allowed to spread naturally in drifts. A lovely effect could be achieved by native planting alone. However, to increase the seasons of interest, other plants have been included.

Primula vulgaris

Primula vulgaris

Site

This border is suitable for an area of light to medium shade, with a well-drained but moisture-retentive soil. The shape illustrated would be particularly suitable for a bed surrounding a tree. It could also be easily adapted for other shady areas of different shapes. Thorough ground preparation is vital as the approach is informal. Plants are included which will spread naturally by suckers, seed or rhizomes so it is important to clear the border of any perennial weeds before planting. Once the plants are established it will be more difficult to eradicate any weeds which are deeply rooted.

Plants and planting

Two different evergreen shrubs have been included which will provide form throughout the year. *Sarcococca hookeriana* var. *digyna* has the added attraction of white flowers with a pervasive scent in the winter months, followed by round black berries. It will spread naturally by its suckering habit.

Ruscus aculeatus (butcher's broom) is a native plant with a spiky appearance. An interesting plant, the 'leaves' are in fact adaptations of the stem which are termed cladodes. On closer inspection, tiny scale-like leaves may be seen on the cladodes and star-shaped flowers in the spring.

Neither of these evergreen shrubs requires any regular pruning.

The spring flowers should be planted in large drifts and allowed to spread naturally. Plant the rhizomes of *Anemone nemorosa* in early autumn,

Ruscus aculeatus

Anemone nemorosa

Pulmonaria saccharata

5cm (2in) deep and 10cm (4in) apart. They will naturalize readily by rhizomes and should be allowed to carpet the ground. Masses of star-shaped white flowers with yellow anthers will be produced in spring amongst deeply divided foliage. *Anemone nemorosa* 'Robinsoniana' is a cultivar which has slightly larger flowers of a lavender blue.

Primroses and violets are familiar spring-flowering native plants, which will spread naturally through the borders.

Pulmonaria saccharata has attractive leaves which are spotted with a silver-white. In spring sprays of flowers open pink and then turn to blue.

Doronicum pardalianches will give a splash of bright yellow with its daisy-like flowers.

Again, this will spread of its own accord.

Dicentra spectabilis carries the flowering interest on into early summer. Unusual, pendent, heart-shaped flowers are formed in graceful arches amongst delicate, fern-like foliage. The

Dicentra spectabilis

species has attractive pink and white flowers against mid-green foliage which has a bronze tinge as it unfurls, whilst the cultivar 'Alba', as its name implies, has pure white flowers against lighter, almost lime green foliage. Being a clump-forming plant it will contrast in form with the spreading plants.

Autumn interest is provided by the Japanese anemones. *Anemone* × *hybrida* 'Honorine Jobert' is a white cultivar and *Anemone hupehensis* a pale pink species with saucer-shaped flowers held on tall stalks. Leave these on over winter to protect the plants, and cut back in the spring.

Alternative plants

The selection chosen for this border only represents a small number of the range of plants suitable for a shady area. Others include:

Polygonatum multiflorum (Solomon's seal)
Lamium maculatum
Convallaria majalis (lily of the valley)
Brunnera macrophylla (Siberian bugloss)
Trillium grandiflorum (wake-robin)

Alchemilla mollis (lady's mantle)
Epimedium perralderianum
Ajuga reptans (bugle)
Prunus laurocerasus 'Otto Luyken'
Hostas
Hellebores
Ribes odoratum (buffalo currant)
Digitalis purpurea (foxglove)
Vincas (periwinkle)
Mahonia aquifolium (Oregon grape)
Hydrangeas
Oxalis acetosella (wood sorrel)
Arum italicum 'Pictum'

This border will be relatively easy to look after, once established, as long as the ground has been well prepared initially. Once planted, spread a thick layer of a mulch, such as bark chippings, over it to provide the protective environment that a woodland edge would naturally have. Top up this mulch every year in early spring. The idea is to enjoy the natural means of propagation of each plant, whether clump-forming or widely spreading, and to allow this to take place without rigidly confining growth. In other words, work hard with the preparation and then sit back and enjoy.

Four Courtyard Designs

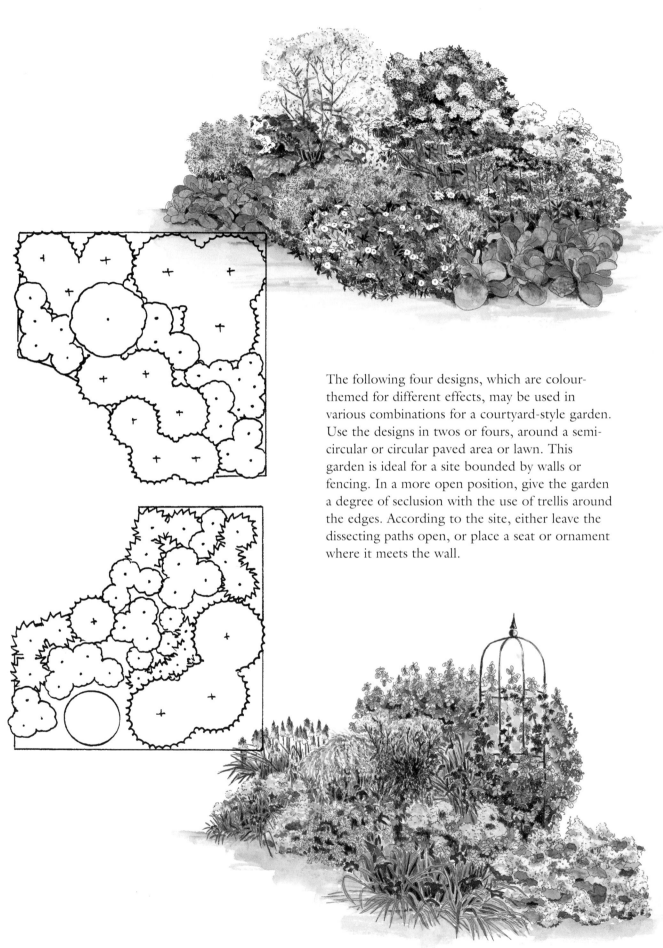

The following four designs, which are colour-
themed for different effects, may be used in
various combinations for a courtyard-style garden.
Use the designs in twos or fours, around a semi-
circular or circular paved area or lawn. This
garden is ideal for a site bounded by walls or
fencing. In a more open position, give the garden
a degree of seclusion with the use of trellis around
the edges. According to the site, either leave the
dissecting paths open, or place a seat or ornament
where it meets the wall.

Selected plants:

1. *Griselinia littoralis* 'Variegata' x 3
2. *Salvia officinalis* 'Icterina'
3. *Hemerocallis* 'Stafford' x 6 (daylily)
4. *Alchemilla mollis* x 8 (lady's mantle)
5. *Kniphofia* 'Royal Standard' x 3
6. *Asparagus officinalis* x 3 (asparagus)
7. *Papaver orientale* 'Allegro' x 3
8. *Foeniculum vulgare* 'Purpureum' x 3 (bronze fennel)
9. *Crocosmia* 'Lucifer' x 5
10. *Thalictrum lucidum* x 5
11. *Tropaeolum speciosum* (flame creeper)

Hot Reds and Cool Greens

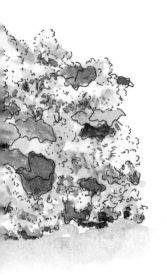

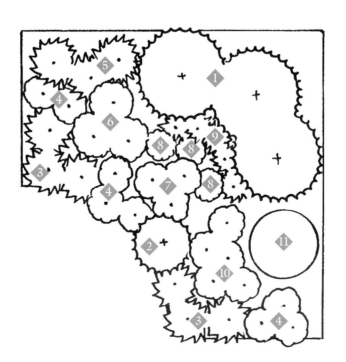

N ←

Scale 1:50

Hot Reds and Cool Greens

The strong red colour scheme of this eye-catching bed creates a dramatic effect. Foliage features highly, too, as many of these red-flowering perennials have spiky leaves. This theme is carried throughout with different groups of plants and is offset by a variety of soft feathery foliage and flowers in greens, creamy-yellows and bronze.

Avoid crowding the different red-flowering plants together, as they are shown to best advantage when the fresh green foliage plants can be seen behind as a backdrop.

Plants and planting

Prepare the bed for planting (see page 10) and start with the three large *Griselinia littoralis* 'Variegata', which will form a backdrop. This shrub is an evergreen with oval leaves of green variegated with cream, which will lighten the appearance of the bed. In colder areas provide some protection for these shrubs.

Tropaeolum speciosum is an herbaceous climber, and will need support, such as an obelisk or willow wigwam. It will twine around the support and produce a vivid display of scarlet nasturtium flowers in the summer.

In front of the backdrop shrubs, plant a long drift of *Crocosmia* 'Lucifer' which, in late summer, has tall spikes of bright red flowers held amongst and above narrow, fresh green foliage.

Further spikes of flowers are produced by clumps of *Kniphofia* 'Royal Standard'. This familiar 'red hot poker' has scarlet and yellow flowers in late summer and strappy, grass-like foliage. Plant a group of three *Hemerocallis* 'Stafford' in the two corners. Sword-like pale green leaves will start emerging in late winter to early spring, followed by the spectacular lily-like flowers in the summer. These are bright red with contrasting yellow throats and only last a day

Tropaeolum speciosum

each, hence their common name, daylily.

As a contrast to the spiky foliage and hot red colours, plant drifts and groups of the softer perennials in between. *Thalictrum lucidum* is tall-growing, with glossy leaves composed of numerous leaflets and feathery heads of greenish-yellow flowers. *Asparagus officinalis* provides a tall feature to balance the height of the obelisk. Often grown for the edible shoots or spears, asparagus also has very attractive, fern-like foliage. *Alchemilla mollis*

Hemerocallis 'Stafford'

Hemerocallis 'Stafford'

has rounded, pale green leaves with crinkled edges, and greenish-yellow frothy flowers to spill over the edges. *Foeniculum vulgare* 'Purpureum', or bronze fennel, also has soft, ferny foliage and the deep colour will complement the reds.

Salvia officinalis 'Icterina' is a low-growing shrub for the front of the bed. The variegated green and yellow foliage provides a setting for one of the most spectacular of the red flowers – *Papaver orientale* 'Allegro'. Plump, rounded flower buds open in early summer to reveal large, bright scarlet flowers and paper-like petals with dark central markings.

Aftercare

- Apply an annual mulch of well-rotted manure or compost in the spring
- In colder areas the kniphofias will require some winter protection. Cover the crowns with straw over the colder months
- The fennel will self-seed readily. Whilst very attractive, you may wish to prevent too many seedlings by removing flowerheads before any seed is produced. Deadhead the other perennials once the flowers are faded
- Cut back dead stems in the autumn

Papaver orientale

Selected plants:

1. *Ceanothus × delileanus* 'Gloire de Versailles'
2. *Potentilla fruticosa* 'Goldfinger'
3. *Ceratostigma willmottianum* x 3
4. *Euonymus fortunei* 'Emerald 'n' Gold' x 6
5. *Achillea filipendulina* 'Gold Plate' x 5
6. *Echinops ritro* 'Veitch's Blue' x 3
7. *Achillea* 'Coronation Gold' x 3
8. *Salvia × sylvestris* 'Mainacht' x 7
9. *Potentilla recta* 'Warrenii' x 3
10. *Miscanthus sinensis* 'Zebrinus' x 6

Blues and Yellows

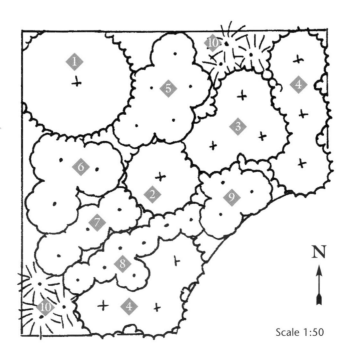

N

Scale 1:50

Blues and Yellows

This bed is a mixture of shrubs and perennials which flower mainly in the summer. Blue and yellow tend to bring out the best in each other – the blue intensifies the yellow, and vice versa, making a simple, yet effective colour scheme.

Plants and planting

Once the bed has been prepared ready for planting, set out the shrubs first. *Ceanothus × delileanus* 'Gloire de Versailles' is a deciduous shrub with pale, powder-blue flowers from mid-summer to autumn. Plant this for a substantial bushy cornerpiece. *Euonymus* 'Emerald 'n' Gold' is a lower-growing evergreen shrub and groups of

Potentilla fruticosa 'Goldfinger'

***Achillea filipendulina* 'Gold Plate'**

The perennials can be planted next, starting with the taller ones towards the back of the bed. *Achillea filipendulina* 'Gold Plate' grows tall and brings a horizontal line of flattened, golden-yellow flowerheads above divided, ferny foliage. *Echinops ritro* 'Veitch's Blue' is another tall plant with spiky foliage and globe-like steel blue flowerheads in late summer, which are much loved by bees. This contrasts with another line of horizontal flowers of *Achillea* 'Coronation Gold'. This is slightly smaller than the other achillea, and has bright golden flowers above silvery foliage. An upright form in front of these is provided by *Salvia × sylvestris* 'Mainacht'. Plant these in a long drift to display the spikes of violet-blue flowers in early summer. *Potentilla recta* 'Warrenii' is an herbaceous potentilla, with the foliage dying back over winter. The flowers are yellow and similar to the shrubby potentilla, but the plant is lower growing, carrying on the theme in a different form. Two groups of grasses provide further upright features, the tall, narrow foliage of *Miscanthus sinensis* 'Zebrinus' being interestingly striped with bands of yellow.

Echinops ritro **'Veitch's Blue': close-up of a flowerhead**

these planted at the corners will make an attractive edging of green and golden variegated foliage. For bright yellow flowers over a long flowering period from late spring to autumn, plant *Potentilla fruticosa* 'Goldfinger' and next to this a group of *Ceratostigma willmottianum*, a bright blue flowering shrub. They are more effective planted in a group, and in the winter will provide a brown twiggy framework, along with the potentilla.

Aftercare

1 Mulch the bed in spring with a layer of well-rotted manure or compost.
2 Provide support for the taller perennials, such as achillea and echinops, with twiggy pea sticks.
3 Leave the attractive seedheads of achillea, echinops and miscanthus over winter, and cut back in the spring.
4 Prune the ceratostigmas in the spring, cutting back to strong healthy buds.

Selected plants:

1. *Olearia × haastii* x 3
2. *Artemesia* 'Powis Castle' x 6
3. *Convolvulus cneorum* x 3
4. *Bergenia* 'Silberlicht' x 8

5. *Thalictrum aquilegiifolium* var. *album* x 7
6. *Leucanthemum × superbum* (*Chrysanthemum × superbum*) x 5 (shasta daisy)
7. *Crambe cordifolia*

White and Silver

N

Scale 1:50

White and Silver

The white and silver colour scheme of this bed gives a light and airy feel. If you like sitting out in the summer evenings, or dining outdoors, this bed would make an appropriate setting. As dusk approaches, the white flowers will appear almost luminescent, and stand out dramatically while other colours fade into the background.

Site and soil

Choose a sunny, south-facing aspect for this bed. A well-drained soil is essential, so the addition of coarse sand or grit may be necessary. Also, incorporate a gritty mixture into the planting holes to give each plant a good start.

Plants and planting

Plant the three *Olearia × hastii* first of all. These are rounded, medium-sized, evergreen shrubs, which become covered with a mass of small white daisy flowers in the summer. The foliage is dark green on top, and grey underneath. These, and several other plants for this bed, have fragrant flowers and foliage, making an even better setting for an outdoor seating area.

Two groups of slightly lower-growing sub-shrubs also give form to this bed. *Artemesia* 'Powis Castle' has fragrant, finely divided, silver foliage. It is grown mainly for the foliage alone, but also has heads of yellow flowers in the summer. Another group of silver foliage plants soften the corner of the bed with their sprawling shapes. The leaves of *Convolvulus cneorum* are covered with tiny hairs which give a silky, silvery appearance, and in the summer pink, furled buds open to funnel-shaped white flowers with yellow centres.

As a contrast, dark green, fleshy leaves fill the other corners. *Bergenia* 'Silberlicht' is an evergreen, herbaceous perennial with upright stems holding clusters of silvery-white flowers which become tinged pink with age and, while most of the other plants are summer flowering, this provides some

Convolvulus cneorum

Bergenia 'Silberlicht'

spring interest. The familiar, cheerful shasta daisy, *Leucanthemum × superbum*, bears large, white, yellow-centred flowers on tall dark green stems. They form a drift through the bed, carrying on the daisy theme from the olearias, but on a larger scale.

Complete the bed with soft, airy forms.

A drift of another herbaceous perennial, *Thalictrum aquilegiifolium* var. *album*, has grey-green ferny foliage and heads of feathery white flowers. A single specimen of *Crambe cordifolia* provides an impressive form, reaching up to 2m (6ft 6in) high, with tall stems rising from the large, dark green foliage, topped with clouds of tiny white flowers.

Aftercare

Very little pruning is required for the shrubs in this bed and routine maintenance – cutting out any dead, damaged or diseased wood – may be carried out at any time. Any growth which has been damaged over winter should be cut out in late spring. To keep a more compact habit for the artemesias, they may be clipped in mid-spring.

Support is required for taller perennials such as the shasta daisies. If these are deadheaded after flowering, they may produce another, smaller flush of flowers.

Selected plants:

1. *Fatsia japonica* (Japanese aralia)
2. *Polygonatum × hybridum* x 3 (Solomon's seal)
3. *Helleborus argutifolius* x 6 (Corsican hellebore)
4. *Hosta crispula*
5. *Alchemilla mollis* x 6 (lady's mantle)
6. *Ophiopogon planiscapus* 'Nigrescens' x 10
7. *Polystichum setiferum* x 7 (soft shield fern)
8. *Hosta sieboldiana* var. *elegans*
9. *Hosta lancifolia*

Sophisticated Foliage

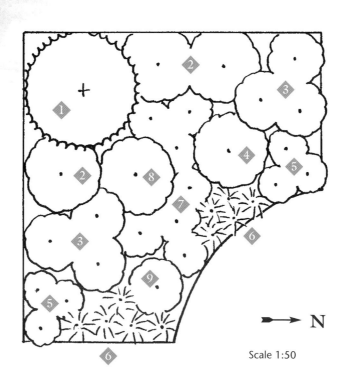

N

Scale 1:50

Sophisticated Foliage

We often buy plants just for their flowers but, when you consider foliage alone, some interesting and pleasing effects can be created and if the plants flower as well, this is just an added bonus. This bed consists mainly of green, making a garden of calm and reflection, or an oasis of green amongst brighter coloured beds. Large glossy leaves contrast with finely divided ferns. Rounded foliage contrasts with grassy foliage. The effects will be heightened after rainfall, with the foliage gleaming and glistening.

Most of these plants require moisture-retentive yet well-drained soil and this bed should be situated in an area of light shade. Improve the soil with the addition of plenty of organic matter during initial preparation.

Plants and planting

Plant the exotic-looking *Fatsia japonica* as a cornerpiece. It will bring a tropical look with its large, luxuriant and glossy foliage and produces unusual, rounded, white flowers in the autumn. It is far hardier than it looks, but may need some protection over winter in colder areas.

Most ferns require damp conditions, but soft shield fern (*Polystichum setiferum*) will tolerate slightly drier conditions. The soil should still be humus-rich and moisture-retentive. The fine fronds of this fern will give all year interest.

Two groups of *Helleborus argutifolius* add further architectural interest with dark green, deeply lobed leaves and, in the spring, they produce stems of cup-shaped, apple-green flowers.

Fatsia japonica

Polystichum setiferum

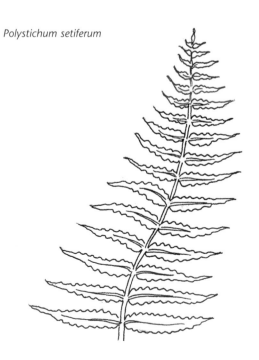

Fatsia japonica

Hosta crispula

Three bold hostas are included as feature plants. There is a great variety of hostas available, with different sizes, variegations and shaped leaves. They all have gentle spires of white or lilac flowers in the summer. *Hosta sieboldiana* var. *elegans* is a large-growing hosta with big, deeply-ribbed, heart-shaped blue-green leaves. *H. crispula* has wavy-edged foliage with white margins, while *H. lancifolia* has narrower, lance-shaped foliage.

Three plants of *Polygonatum* × *hybridum* provide a horizontal line for the picture. These have arching stems of narrow leaves and pendulous green-white flowers.

Two different groups of plants are used for the edging. *Ophiopogon planiscapus* 'Nigrescens' has a grassy effect with its unusual, almost black, strappy foliage which will contrast well with the fresh green foliage and yellow-green frothy flowers of *Alchemilla mollis.*

Aftercare

It is vital to keep up the organic content of this bed, so regular mulches of compost or bark are a must. Little pruning is necessary but, should the fatsia require any cutting back, do this in the spring.

Hostas are very prone to attack by slugs, which are likely to be active as dusk approaches. One method of deterring them is to mulch around each hosta with a layer of grit, rather than compost. Otherwise, keep an eye out for damage – with just three plants it may be possible to keep the slugs under control by picking off by hand.

Hosta sieboldiana

Photographic credits:

Anthony Bailey: pp. 4, 5 and 9

Dave Bevan: p. 103

S. E. Marshall & Co Ltd: p. 82

Eric Sawford: pp. 21, 22, 23, 25, 28 (bottom), 33, 36, 39, 43, 44 (bottom), 49, 50 (top left and bottom right), 51, 54, 56 (bottom), 60–1, 64, 66 (top), 67, 71, 83, 87–9, 95, 97, 105 (top), 109 (bottom), 112, 118, 125 (top), 128–9 and 138

Jenny Shukman: pp. vi, 7, 20, 28 (top), 29, 32, 37, 38, 43 (top), 44 (top), 50 (bottom) 55, 56 (top), 70–1, 74–5, 80, 90, 94, 95 (top) 96, 100, 104, 105 (bottom), 108, 109 (top), 112, 113, 116–17, 125 (bottom) 137 and 139

Julian Slatcher: pp. 65, 66 (middle and bottom)

Unwins Seeds Ltd: p. 81

About the Author

Jenny Shukman has enjoyed working in horticulture for many years. A year's practical training led to a post as head gardener for a ten acre private garden. Following that, she worked for the National Trust at Polesden Lacey, Surrey, a beautiful garden with the added bonus of spectacular views over the North Downs.

Jenny's current work revolves around tutoring in horticulture and running her own garden design business. Commissions are mainly for smaller, private gardens, but have included a garden open to the public in Cathedral Close, Salisbury.

Horticultural qualifications include an OCA award in Garden Design, and the RHS Diploma in Horticulture, for which Jenny received the Chittenden award.

Index

*Page numbers in **bold** include illustrations of plants.*

TITLES AVAILABLE FROM
GMC Publications

BOOKS

WOODCARVING

The Art of the Woodcarver	*GMC Publications*
Carving Architectural Detail in Wood: The Classical Tradition	
	Frederick Wilbur
Carving Birds & Beasts	*GMC Publications*
Carving Nature: Wildlife Studies in Wood	*Frank Fox-Wilson*
Carving Realistic Birds	*David Tippey*
Decorative Woodcarving	*Jeremy Williams*
Elements of Woodcarving	*Chris Pye*
Essential Tips for Woodcarvers	*GMC Publications*
Essential Woodcarving Techniques	*Dick Onians*
Further Useful Tips for Woodcarvers	*GMC Publications*
Lettercarving in Wood: A Practical Course	*Chris Pye*
Making & Using Working Drawings for Realistic Model Animals	
	Basil F. Fordham
Power Tools for Woodcarving	*David Tippey*
Practical Tips for Turners & Carvers	*GMC Publications*
Relief Carving in Wood: A Practical Introduction	*Chris Pye*
Understanding Woodcarving	*GMC Publications*
Understanding Woodcarving in the Round	*GMC Publications*
Useful Techniques for Woodcarvers	*GMC Publications*
Wildfowl Carving – Volume 1	*Jim Pearce*
Wildfowl Carving – Volume 2	*Jim Pearce*
Woodcarving: A Complete Course	*Ron Butterfield*
Woodcarving: A Foundation Course	*Zoë Gertner*
Woodcarving for Beginners	*GMC Publications*
Woodcarving Tools & Equipment Test Reports	*GMC Publications*
Woodcarving Tools, Materials & Equipment	*Chris Pye*

WOODTURNING

Adventures in Woodturning	*David Springett*
Bert Marsh: Woodturner	*Bert Marsh*
Bowl Turning Techniques Masterclass	*Tony Boase*
Colouring Techniques for Woodturners	*Jan Sanders*
Contemporary Turned Wood: New Perspectives in a Rich Tradition	
	Ray Leier, Jan Peters & Kevin Wallace
The Craftsman Woodturner	*Peter Child*
Decorative Techniques for Woodturners	*Hilary Bowen*
Fun at the Lathe	*R.C. Bell*
Further Useful Tips for Woodturners	*GMC Publications*
Illustrated Woodturning Techniques	*John Hunnex*
Intermediate Woodturning Projects	*GMC Publications*
Keith Rowley's Woodturning Projects	*Keith Rowley*
Practical Tips for Turners & Carvers	*GMC Publications*
Turning Green Wood	*Michael O'Donnell*
Turning Miniatures in Wood	*John Sainsbury*
Turning Pens and Pencils	*Kip Christensen & Rex Burningham*
Understanding Woodturning	*Ann & Bob Phillips*
Useful Techniques for Woodturners	*GMC Publications*
Useful Woodturning Projects	*GMC Publications*
Woodturning: Bowls, Platters, Hollow Forms, Vases, Vessels, Bottles, Flasks, Tankards, Plates	*GMC Publications*

Woodturning: A Foundation Course (New Edition)	*Keith Rowley*
Woodturning: A Fresh Approach	*Robert Chapman*
Woodturning: An Individual Approach	*Dave Regester*
Woodturning: A Source Book of Shapes	*John Hunnex*
Woodturning Jewellery	*Hilary Bowen*
Woodturning Masterclass	*Tony Boase*
Woodturning Techniques	*GMC Publications*
Woodturning Tools & Equipment Test Reports	*GMC Publications*
Woodturning Wizardry	*David Springett*

WOODWORKING

Bird Boxes and Feeders for the Garden	*Dave Mackenzie*
Complete Woodfinishing	*Ian Hosker*
David Charlesworth's Furniture-Making Techniques	
	David Charlesworth
The Encyclopedia of Joint Making	*Terrie Noll*
Furniture & Cabinetmaking Projects	*GMC Publications*
Furniture-Making Projects for the Wood Craftsman	*GMC Publications*
Furniture-Making Techniques for the Wood Craftsman	*GMC Publications*
Furniture Projects	*Rod Wales*
Furniture Restoration (Practical Crafts)	*Kevin Jan Bonner*
Furniture Restoration and Repair for Beginners	*Kevin Jan Bonner*
Furniture Restoration Workshop	*Kevin Jan Bonner*
Green Woodwork	*Mike Abbott*
Kevin Ley's Furniture Projects	*Kevin Ley*
Making & Modifying Woodworking Tools	*Jim Kingshott*
Making Chairs and Tables	*GMC Publications*
Making Classic English Furniture	*Paul Richardson*
Making Little Boxes from Wood	*John Bennett*
Making Shaker Furniture	*Barry Jackson*
Making Woodwork Aids and Devices	*Robert Wearing*
Minidrill: Fifteen Projects	*John Everett*
Pine Furniture Projects for the Home	*Dave Mackenzie*
Practical Scrollsaw Patterns	*John Everett*
Router Magic: Jigs, Fixtures and Tricks to Unleash your Router's Full Potential	*Bill Hylton*
Routing for Beginners	*Anthony Bailey*
The Scrollsaw: Twenty Projects	*John Everett*
Sharpening: The Complete Guide	*Jim Kingshott*
Sharpening Pocket Reference Book	*Jim Kingshott*
Simple Scrollsaw Projects	*GMC Publications*
Space-Saving Furniture Projects	*Dave Mackenzie*
Stickmaking: A Complete Course	*Andrew Jones & Clive George*
Stickmaking Handbook	*Andrew Jones & Clive George*
Test Reports: *The Router* and *Furniture & Cabinetmaking*	
	GMC Publications
Veneering: A Complete Course	*Ian Hosker*
Woodfinishing Handbook (Practical Crafts)	*Ian Hosker*
Woodworking with the Router: Professional Router Techniques any Woodworker can Use	
	Bill Hylton & Fred Matlack
The Workshop	*Jim Kingshott*